Nancy Graves: Recent Works

Nancy Graves: Recent Works

Curated by David Yager

Essays by
E. A. Carmean, Jr.
and
Robert C. Morgan

Conversation with Nancy Graves
by David Yager

Fine Arts Gallery

University of Maryland, Baltimore County

COVER: *Send Ups of Venerable Traditions* (detail), 1990

SCHEDULE OF THE EXHIBITION

Fine Arts Gallery
University of Maryland,
Baltimore County
Catonsville, Maryland
February 18 - March 27, 1993

The Lamont Gallery
The Frederick R. Mayer Art Center
Phillips Exeter Academy
Exeter, New Hampshire
September 17 - October 25, 1993

The Chrysler Museum
Norfolk, Virginia
February 26 - April 24, 1994

The Jacksonville Art Museum
Jacksonville, Florida
June 1 - July 31, 1994

Designed by Jane Polanka

Edited by Antonia Gardner

Photography by Ken Cohen
(except where otherwise indicated)

Printed by John D. Lucas Printers,
Baltimore, Maryland

Library of Congress Catalogue Card Number
92-75184

ISBN 0-9624565-3-5

Contents

Preface

The Nancy Graves exhibition is one of the few projects in my life to fit together on its own strength and content. Throughout its entirety the project has remained intact, continuously growing with love and intensity, and gaining a new base of knowledge as the opening date moves closer to reality. This has been the case with *Nancy Graves: Recent Works.*

In the art world, Nancy's work has sometimes fallen between a number of cracks, and has sometimes not received the recognition it has deserved. This exhibition attempts to bring a large body of recent work together, and is accompanied by a catalogue with essays, so one is able to have a more personal view of this new work.

As a curator, my experience working alongside Nancy will influence my thought process forever. She is a remarkable artist, thinker, humanitarian and now a friend.

I have enjoyed putting this travelling exhibition together and hope you can enjoy viewing it with much of the same active enthusiasm.

Thank you, Nancy.

David Yager, 1993
Curator, *Nancy Graves: Recent Works*

Acknowledgments

The rare pleasure afforded the Fine Arts Gallery by having the opportunity to collaborate with Nancy Graves in bringing her most recent works to the public can not be underestimated. We have been most fortunate to work with an artist who can be both gracious with her time as well as energetic and attentive to the various details surrounding an exhibition project. Her commitment to this exhibition from its inception to its final form is an eloquent example of her understanding of the educational process and its value to the individual. We offer to her our heartfelt thanks and gratitude.

For their continuing support of the Fine Arts Gallery and invaluable assistance in the implementation of this project and many others, we wish to acknowledge the important contributions made by the following individuals at the University of Maryland, Baltimore County: Our appreciation goes to Freeman Hrabowski, Interim President of the University, Arthur Pittenger, Dean of Arts and Sciences, Mark Behm, Vice President for Administrative Affairs, and Leland Beitel, Associate Vice President for Administrative Affairs.

The catalogue that accompanys this exhibition has been made possible only by enlisting the knowledge and expertise of the following people. For their efforts we want to express our appreciation and thanks: E. A. Carmean, Jr., and Robert C. Morgan for their insightful and informative essays on Nancy Graves's work and its sources; Antonia Gardner for balancing the many grammatical nuances and factual information in editing the catalogue; Jane Polanka for her abilities in designing the content and visual context of the catalogue; and Monika Graves, who assisted in the organization of the numerous parts of this document as well as the project overall and its travelling schedule.

We would also like to thank Donald Saff and Saff Tech Arts for their expertise and knowledge in the fabrication and installation of Ms. Graves's works; Janie Samuels, Assistant to Nancy Graves, for her consistent ability to research and furnish necessary information and background knowledge in all aspects of Ms. Graves's work; and Knoedler & Company in New York and Eliza Beghe in particular for their assistance with this project. Finally, our appreciation goes out to Trinket Clark of the Chrysler Museum and all the individuals representing institutions who enabled this exhibition to reach audiences throughout the Atlantic seaboard.

David Yager
Director

Symmes Gardner
Coordinator of Exhibitions

On Visual Complexity in Nancy Graves's New Works

E. A. Carmean, Jr.

THE POINT HERE, I THINK, IS THE INTERFACING OF THE TWO; MY PAINTING WITH ITS INCREASED PLANARITY, NUMBERS OF CANVASES, AND THE ADDITION OF SCULPTURAL ELEMENTS HAS BECOME MORE SCULPTURAL, AND THE SCULPTURE IN TURN MORE VARIED IN SURFACE INCIDENT: TEXTURE AND DETAIL.[1]

NANCY GRAVES

Beginning with the first exhibition of her *Camel* sculptures at New York's Graham Gallery in 1968, Nancy Graves has been recognized as an important figure in post-1960s art.[2] Best known as a sculptor, Graves has also worked in relief, painting, watercolor, drawing, and printmaking, although these other media have often had an identity somewhat apart from her central focus. With her most recent work, beginning in 1990, these disparate concerns have come much closer—particularly painting and sculpture and especially relief, which structurally rests between them.

This merging is due in part to shifts made in her own formal vocabulary and in part to the introduction of new elements into her repertory of compositional components. Key among this latter group of forms are elements derived from works by other artists, forms that provide Graves with an expanded sculptural and pictorial range.

Almost without exception, Graves's art has a specific degree of realism about it, in the sense that the forms she employs derive from things we encounter in the real world. Certainly the early *Camels* and *Fossils* depend directly upon things taken from nature itself, and her contemporary two-dimensional works of this period—*Maps* paintings and drawings, for example—are also created in a one-to-nearly-one correspondence with actual objects.

Around 1980, when Graves shifted her sculpture to a format of a welded structure, this realism continued, but more in the identity of the individual components rather than in the overall character of the work itself. Here, by casting objects directly from nature—a fern, for example—Graves allows her compositional components to carry forward their origins in the natural world, but they are ultimately superceded by her larger sculptural concerns. And these larger concerns are essentially abstract. Although some references to realism might still be present in the work's structure in the sense of a natural sway of forms or a forthright, humanlike verticality, these references are achieved by the syntax of the forms, not by any manner of depiction.

Her painting and other two-dimensional work of this same time is largely a separate matter. To be sure, like the sculpture, these works are extraordinarily lyrical; but they are comprised of completely different kinds of elements and structural concerns. Even her two-dimensional works of the late 1980s, which flirt with relief by means of attached sculptural components, still retain an essentially pictorial basis.

Graves's work since 1990 does not change her art but rather shifts its course, and in doing so pushes the differing media into closer correspondence. Her painting, relief, and sculpture share a greater sense of a transparency of the overall composition and a greater layering of the elements within it. The resulting effect is at once one of a greater openness of the whole and at the same time, one of a tighter cohesion of the interwoven elements. Certain new components based in reality also contribute to this shift, most of all those which derive from works by other artists. These latter elements introduce a new visual pacing into Graves's already rich artistic vocabulary.

A Range of Forms

By the end of the last decade, the components in Graves's art, especially her sculpture, were so numerous they could be identified in four general groups: nature, food, tools, and forms derived from the making process itself. Cast from the actual objects, the natural elements include twigs, vines, ferns, bamboo, fungi, leaves, gourds, beans, and cucumbers. Since 1990, Graves has added to this division components cast from sunflowers, bark, bananas, a starfish, horseshoe crabs, fish bones, a sheep's hoof, and a Tyrannosaurus tooth. Some of these are also food, and can be added to earlier elements based on lobsters and crayfish, as well as eggs and sardines, each still in their traditional Japanese packaging. Pretzels appear earlier, recently joined by forms cast from pasta.

The range of components in the tool category is equally broad—except here, in addition to cast forms, Graves also occasionally includes an actual tool in the welded structure of her sculpture. These elements include scissors, doorknobs, fans, eel spears, pitchforks, an abacus, a lawnmower, and a barbecue grill. A stove, basketball nets, wagon yokes, a plow, a windmill, Japanese calendars, and Indonesian puppets have enlarged this grouping in the last three years. The fourth category of process—seen in clamps, steel bars, spills, and casting gatings—has remained unexpanded, except for her use in sculpture of carved frames to suggest painting.

Beyond these significant recent additions, Graves has also introduced forms derived from three new groupings of original sources. Elements cast from architecture include corbels, sheets of Islamic window tracery, the grooved cap of a niche, and Egyptian and Classical Greek capitals. Anatomical components have been derived from a rib cage, teeth, lungs, blood vessels, and bones from a child's jaw as well as a sternum, a scapula, a femur, and vertebrae. Other, created forms include an eye and a breast with a partial shoulder.

Of the recently introduced groups, the most important is a gathering of forms based on other, earlier art. These elements are also more complicated; as in previous forms, some are derived from castings (obviously from replicas), while others are traced and transformed or even recreated. And the range is equally broad, from Egyptian, Assyrian, Greek, and Roman art to the Italian Renaissance to objects from Korea, Japan, Africa, and Australia.

Of course, virtually all artists depend upon other art for instruction, inspiration, or even companionship. During the 1980s Graves made several works that draw on this association, sculpture whose formal shapes directly recall shapes found in older artists' work. For example, her *Nuda* (1984) alludes to Matisse and *Walk* (1983) to Dubuffet. Two sculptures—*Zag* (1983) and *Fought Cight Cockfight* (1984)—are indebted to David Smith, while her *Griddleman* (1985) and *Le Sourire* (1985) are reminiscent of Picasso's sculpture.[3]

Graves's more recent works employing historical works of art depart from this kind of connection. Unlike the previous works, no overt linkage is made through Graves's overall structure. Instead, bits and pieces of earlier artists' creations take up their place within the complex texture of Graves's own abstract composition. Furthermore, despite their origins, these elements have been radically altered by the artist, not only through fragmentation but also by shifts in scale, material, color, and orientation. As Graves notes, "My concern is to find an object, re-examine it, transform it by casting, by juxtaposition, by subordination to the whole, by illogical color."[4]

These historical art elements also introduce another, quite differing aspect of perception. When we look at a cast fern in her sculpture, we know it is a derived object—one transformed from its initial appearance. But we do not know art as objectively. Our perception is temporally altered in our recognition of the component as already existing as art in another work. Thus seeing the *Empress Theodora* mosaic of Ravenna in Graves's new art, we see the original first. We abstractly see it as an art image before questions of transformation or compositional usage enter our experience. In a similar way, while her *Le Sourire* only gradually reveals its indebtedness to Picasso's *Head of a Woman* (1929-30), in the recent work our recognition of a *Laocoön* head is immediate and arresting. These art elements stop our attention, and when several are combined in one work, they cause what might be called a kind of visual stuttering in our understanding of the whole work, a perceptual interference that increases the density and complexity already present in her work.[5]

Three Works

Three recent works serve well to illustrate the changes underway in Graves's paintings, reliefs , and sculpture. The first of these, *Magnetic Plate of Calls and Answers* (1991, fig. A), is a large painting com-

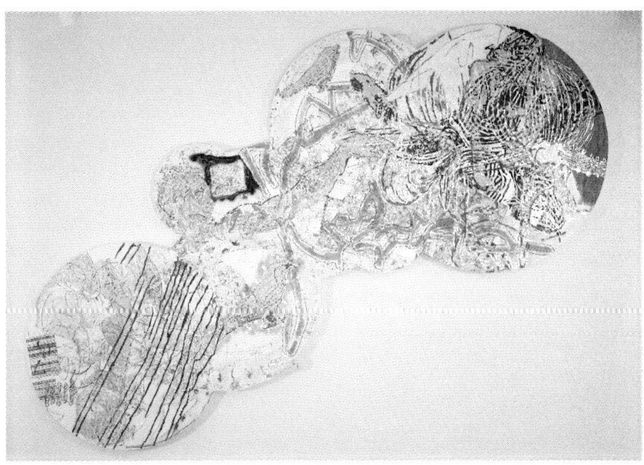

FIG. A. *MAGNETIC PLATE OF CALLS AND ANSWERS*, 1991, OIL, GOLD LEAF ON CANVAS AND ALUCOBOND. 109 X 190"

prised of six flat, intersecting circular fields of varying sizes, its continuous surface rolling upward from the lower left corner. Graves's paint here is (for her) quite translucent and somewhat pale in its overall tonality. In addition to abstract passages and a few plant forms that appear in various places, the dominant elements are drawn from historical art, beginning with two facing pairs of Egyptian heads rendered in the lower, pink-toned circle.

These pharaonic profiles are painted yellow, as is the Egyptian falcon that dominates the adjacent circle. This bird is echoed in two smaller versions, also in yellow; one directly above in a small circle (bordered by a black boxlike shape); the other atop the large, uppermost circle.

The most effective derived images in *Magnetic Plate* are the figures in the center and right of the composition—details drawn from Michelangelo's

Creation of Adam from the Sistine Ceiling. Here painted in pale green, Adam's head and shoulders begin with the upper small circle at the left, his head nearly coincident with the outer limit of this field. Adam's left arm reaches across the central surface, ending slightly within the exterior of the rightmost circle.

God's hand, in gray outlined in royal blue, emerges out of a field of blue and reaches toward that of Adam, while another Adam-derived hand, also in gray-blue, is placed directly above. Interestingly, the figure of God has been rotated clockwise from its orientation on the Sistine Ceiling in such a way that His hand now points upward (rather than horizontally) and seems to mediate between the green and the gray Adam hands.[6]

Despite the transparency Graves uses in rendering Michelangelo's figures, our knowledge of them pulls our attention toward the middle of the painting and locks the circles together (tondo shapes are unstable). Also bonding these fields is a snake element, which sweeps around the second left circle, up around Adam's head, and encloses both the uppermost circle and the small field emerging below. In contradiction to the two-dimensionality of the composition, this snake's profile is coincident with the profile of the canvas shapes, causing a spatial shift as we read its fictive dimensional role simultaneously with the curve of the supporting ground.

The historical art images and the layering translucency of the overall composition of *Magnetic Plate* are shared in one of Graves's recent reliefs, the imposing *Canoptic Legerdemain* (1990, figs. B and C). Seven different derived elements are interwoven in a construction that projects nearly three feet forward from the back plane of its supporting wall. Approached directly from the front, *Canoptic Legerdemain* appears to be a densely packed, irregularly shaped mass (fig. B). But moving to the side view, the work reveals more clearly the complicated layering and spatial jousting of its disparate components (fig. C).

Projecting outward from the upper left back plane is a large, abstracted head, the image taken

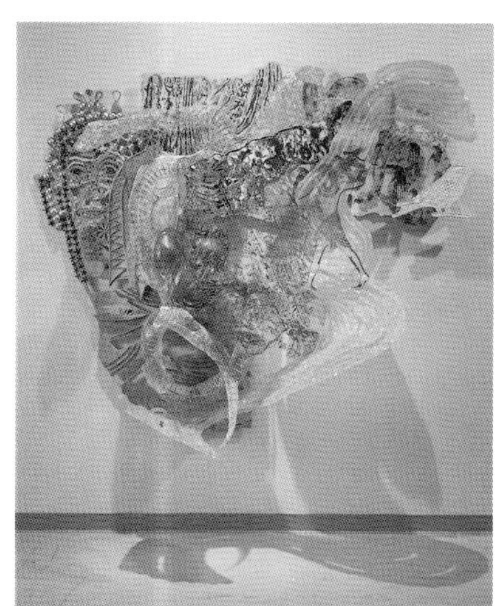

FIG. B.
CANOPTIC LEGERDEMAIN
1990
MIXED MEDIA
78 1/2 x 95 x 35"
(FRONTAL VIEW)

© GRAPHICSTUDIO UNIVERSITY OF FLORIDA.
PHOTO: GEORGE HOLZER

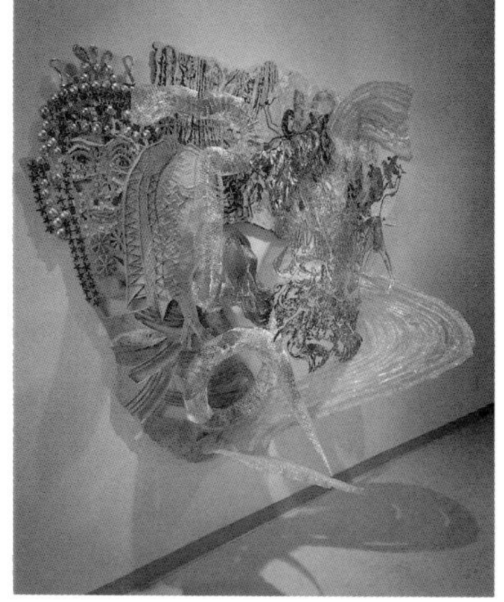

FIG. C.
CANOPTIC LEGERDEMAIN,
(SIDE VIEW)

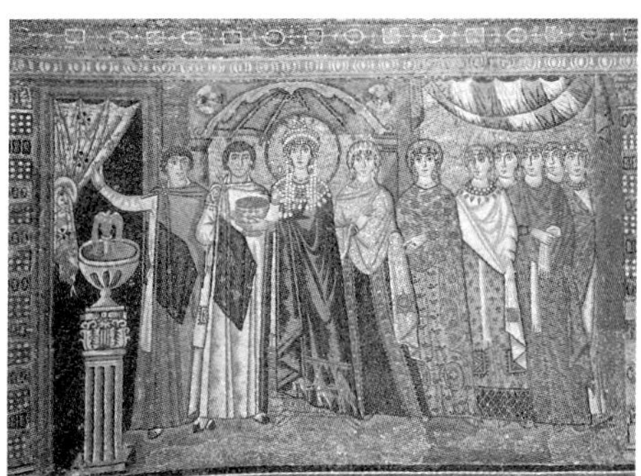

Empress Theodora and Attendants, c. 547 A.D., mosaic, S. Vitale, Ravenna

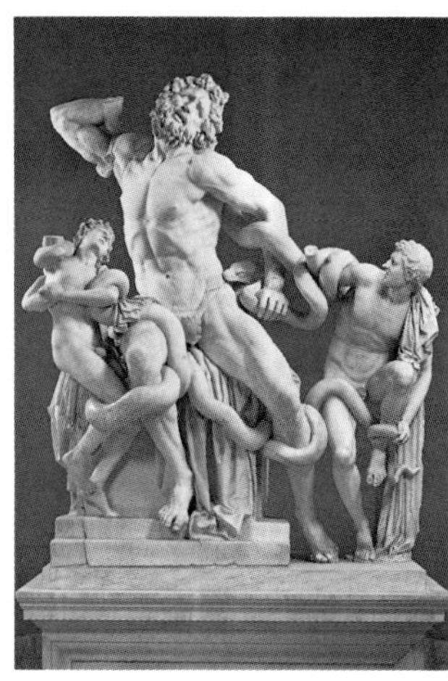

Laocoön, 1st c. A.D., marble, h. 7' Vatican Museums, Rome

from the head of the Empress Theodora in the mosaic from the Altar at San' Vitale in Ravenna. Recreated by Graves, Theodora's face is rendered in rectangular blocks of pink and tan—suggestive of the original's tesserae—and in cut forms of deep red. Graves's whimsy is expressed in Theodora's crown and hanging jewels, presented here by using gold balls and irregular blue stars. At the same time, their dimensionality, however shallow, announces that Graves's structure is one projecting into space from the back, wall plane.

In front of Graves's Theodora is a flat snake shown in profile, reaching upward and curving inward at its head. The profile of the snake overlaps that of an Egyptian fish, which is also aligned in a vertical position. Above this duo we find another snake, rendered three-dimensionally in an open metal mesh. This silver-toned snake twists through the left side of *Canoptic Legerdemain*, its head rising above Theodora, its tail looping around and downward toward the lower compositional center. While this snake was invented by the artist, its origin lies in the twists and turns of the snake in *The Laocoön Group*, especially the head and body between Laocoön and his son at the right.

Graves's Laocoön-inspired snake, with its Hellenistic twists and its nearly transparent mesh formulation finds a counterpoint in an even larger rendering of a swirling wave of water that controls the right portion of the relief. Created in an opaque fiberglass, the wave sweeps inward and down from the upper right, then turning outward and back to the right, broadening its swirl as it projects forward, before twisting again and again as it passes under the loop of the Laocoön snake.

In contrast to these strong forms to the left and right, the forward level of the center is occupied by another historical art image rendered with great subtlety, a pharaonic hunting scene drawn from an Egyptian tomb. (Another Egyptian image, the falcon we have already seen in *Magnetic Plate*, is placed at the composition's right.) Graves's pharaonic relief extends from the upper center—where a hunter lies atop a red Korean carp—to the lower center over an empty back plane and to the right, where the other hunter stands astride the forward projection of the translucent wave.

With this pharaonic relief Graves indicates an even broader transformation of her art sources. Although rendered in *Canoptic Legerdemain* as a relieflike structure, the original work is in fact a fragment of a wall painting, the *Nebamun Hunting Birds* from the Eighteenth Dynasty Tomb of Nebamun at Thebes.

Fowling in the Marshes, 18th Dynasty, Nebamun Tomb, Thebes

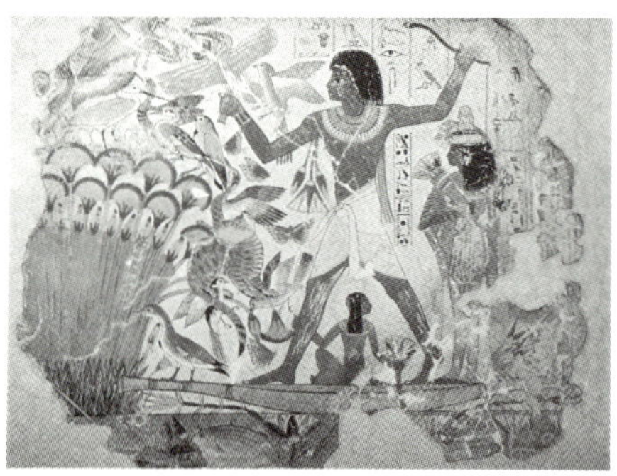

Hunting and Fishing, (detail: *Fish*), 1422-1411 B.C., 15 x 10 1/2" Tomb of Menna, Thebes

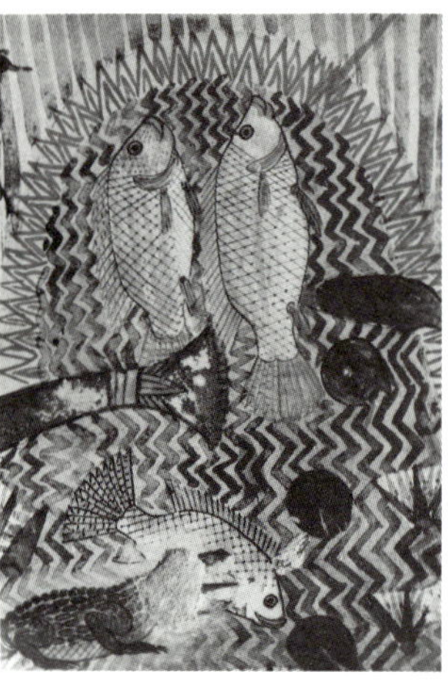

(Graves's vertical fish to the left is also based on a painting at Thebes, slightly earlier, where it is also placed vertically.) Recognizing this Nebamun source also allows us to recognize that the hunter at the upper left is another, but now reversed, image of the original wall image. Slightly reduced in scale from its companion hunter at the right, this reversed figure also lacks the vertical plant massing that the larger translated image shares with the source image. Further comparison with the source indicates that the lower grouping of birds is entirely Graves's own invention.

Graves's transformation of the image (made by a laser cut into sheet metal) turns the origin painting into a relief—but one in which shading is rendered as solid material and the conventional stone surface is present as voided, empty space. Like other elements in this relief, Graves's handling allows an open layering of structure while providing visually arresting imagery.

This mixture of layering, transparency, and historical art imagery is now a salient aspect of Graves's freestanding sculpture as well. Among the largest of these recent works is *Unending Revolution of Venus, Plants, and Pendulum* (1990, figs. D and E), which gathers together twenty-two of her new elements. And despite the greater openness of certain components, it is still necessary to see the sculpture from varying positions to recognize all of the participants in this complex composition.

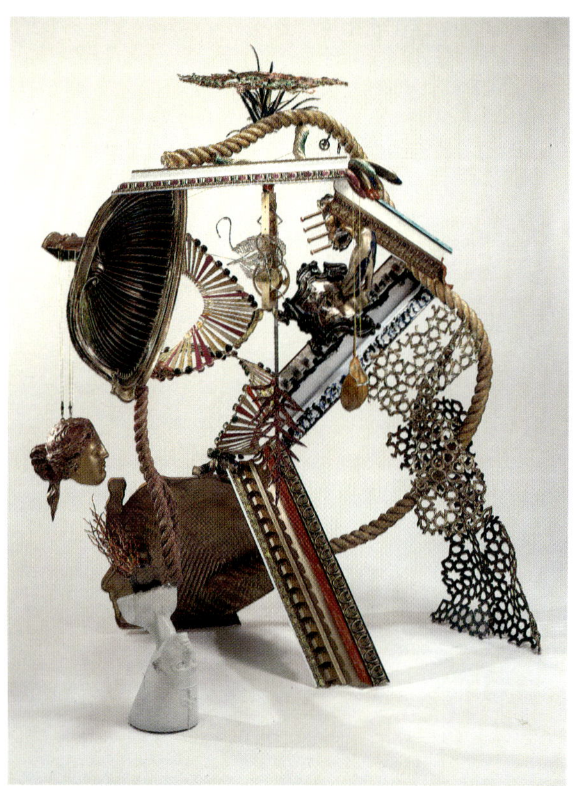

Fig. D. *Unending Revolution of Venus, Plants, and Pendulum*, 1992, bronze, brass, stainless steel, steel, aluminum, and enamel. 97 x 71 1/2 x 56 1/2". © Saff Tech Arts. Photo: George Holzer

One perspective—with the hanging head of Venus to the left—reveals the majority of the cast sculptural elements (fig. D). Crowning the composition is an architectural filigree ornament, held aloft by an aloe plant attached to a piece of cast rope. (Barely visible behind is a piece of cast twine that helps provide structural support.) The rope rests upon a horizontal piece of architectural molding, one of four that zigzag through the sculpture—downward to the right, diagonally back to the left, then diagonally right against to the ground. In turn the cast rope—not unlike Laocoön's snake—twists through this zigzag, bowing outward to the right, before crossing behind the lower architectural element. This rope also passes through architecture, in that the mesh of stars and circles to the right is a folded plane based on Islamic tracery.

Shifting to the left side of this perspective we find other architecture in the solid, ribbed cap of a niche, turned diagonally at the end of the horizontal molding. Twisting off this cap, to the center and down to the molding elements is a swirl of architectural ornament, here in an open striped pattern.

QUEEN NOFRETETE
C. 1360 B.C., LIMESTONE, H.C. 20", STATE MUSEUM, BERLIN

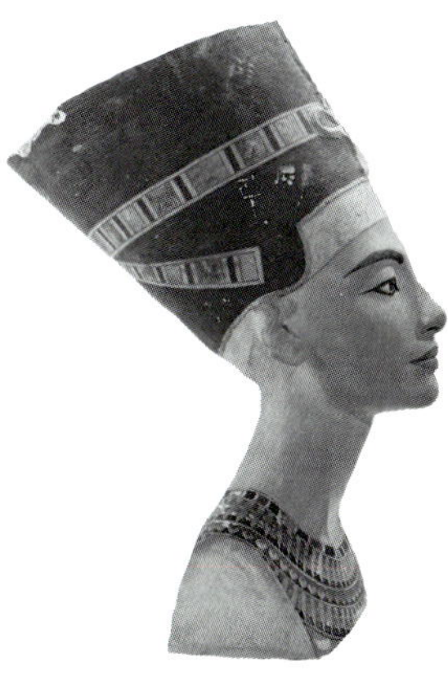

Hanging below the niche cap is the head of Venus, at the far left, and a second piece of cast rope, which turns back up to form an open loop. This curl rests atop an inverted casting of the head and shoulders of Queen Nofretete, here painted a uniform white. This element is perhaps a symbol of Graves's direction in these new works; as she notes, ". . . ideas and elements are reexamined and reinvented, so to speak. [For] some years now I've been trying to stand sculpture on its head—as I did Nefertiti in the Venus sculpture."[7]

Elements at the center of the work are smaller in size, and thus initially more difficult to identify. At the joinings of the upper moldings we find a bunch of cast bananas, while peeking out from behind is the head of Laocoön (with four attached bolts); directly below the bananas is a hand, which is tangent with a framed portion of lower human torso. Further below this grouping is a hanging cast horseshoe crab. To the left of this element is a vertical fern leaf, hanging from a clockworks and a laser-cut stainless steel eye.

Moving around the Venus to another view (fig. E), other components are more clearly recog-

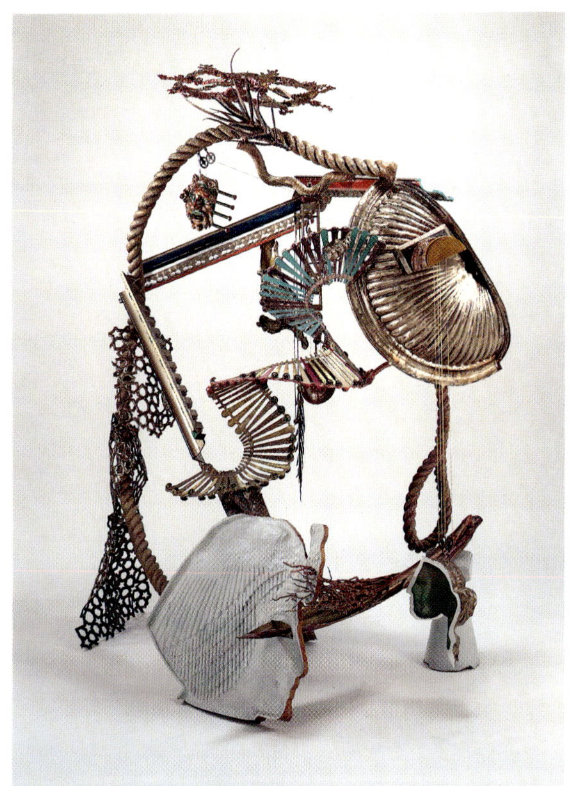

FIG. E. *VENUS* (ALTERNATE VIEW)

nizable, including the Laocoön head, the supporting twine, and the second rope's enclosed loop at the right. At the lower center, painted, like Nofretete, in white, is a head of Ramses, adopted from a wall relief. Piercing through his eye is the end of a cast palm bud, which crosses to the right, to the upper edge of the inverted Nofretete bust. As on the recto, smaller elements are located in the center: a cast capital projects outward from the niche cap and a small foot is placed to its left, in the middle of the upper level of the architectural swirl.

Close attention between the two views illustrated here reveals differing locations for the Laocoön and Venus heads, the fern leaf, and the horseshoe crab, all components attached by brass cables through pulleys. Their shifting positions are not the result of manual adjustment; rather their movements are governed by the clockworks located in the sculpture's center. Indeed, these elements serve as counterbalanced weights to drive this key-wound mechanism. Time measurement itself is indicated by the laser-cut eye (for the hours) and a small aluminum vine (for minutes).

Kinetic sculpture has been a part of modern art since Calder, and over the last decade Graves has made numerous works that employ adjustable components, including *Wheelabout* (1985), where wheels allow the sculpture itself to be easily repositioned.[8] But in *Venus*, the movement of the components adds further to an already intense aesthetic experience, challenging our understanding of previous convention. Along with recent paintings and relief structures, *Venus* and other freestanding works push further by their complex visual pressure toward "turning sculpture on its head."

E. A. Carmean, Jr., is Director of the Memphis Brooks Museum in Memphis, Tennessee. In 1988, as Director of the Fort Worth Art Museum, he organized a travelling retrospective of the painting and sculpture of Nancy Graves and produced a definitive catalogue raisonné of her work.

Notes

References here given thusly—FW—refer to the catalogue raisonné of Graves's sculpture, prepared under the author's direction; *The Sculpture of Nancy Graves* (New York, Hudson Hills, 1987).

1. Nancy Graves letter to E.A. Carmean, June 10, 1992.

2. *The Camels* are FW 1A-E, 2, 3, 4, 6, 8.

3. The Graves's sculpture referred to here are, in order cited, FW 169, 152, 153, 164, 192, 211.

4. *Op. cit.*, n. 1.

5. One of Graves's new historically referenced art works does employ a syntax that is indebted to another work; her *Slaying the Dragon*, 1990, relates directly to the format of Kandinsky's several paintings of *St. George and the Dragon*. In the Graves work, an open cast of Adam's hand appears at the left, where the dragon is placed in Kandinsky's works. In both cases, this kind of arresting attention serves a similar function to "detail," as Graves indicates in the statement quoted in Note 1.

6. A question of color references can be raised here, as the Egyptian color of the dead is yellow, combined with the earth green of Adam and the celestial blue of God.

7. *Op. cit.*, n. 1.

8. *Wheelabout*, FW 225.

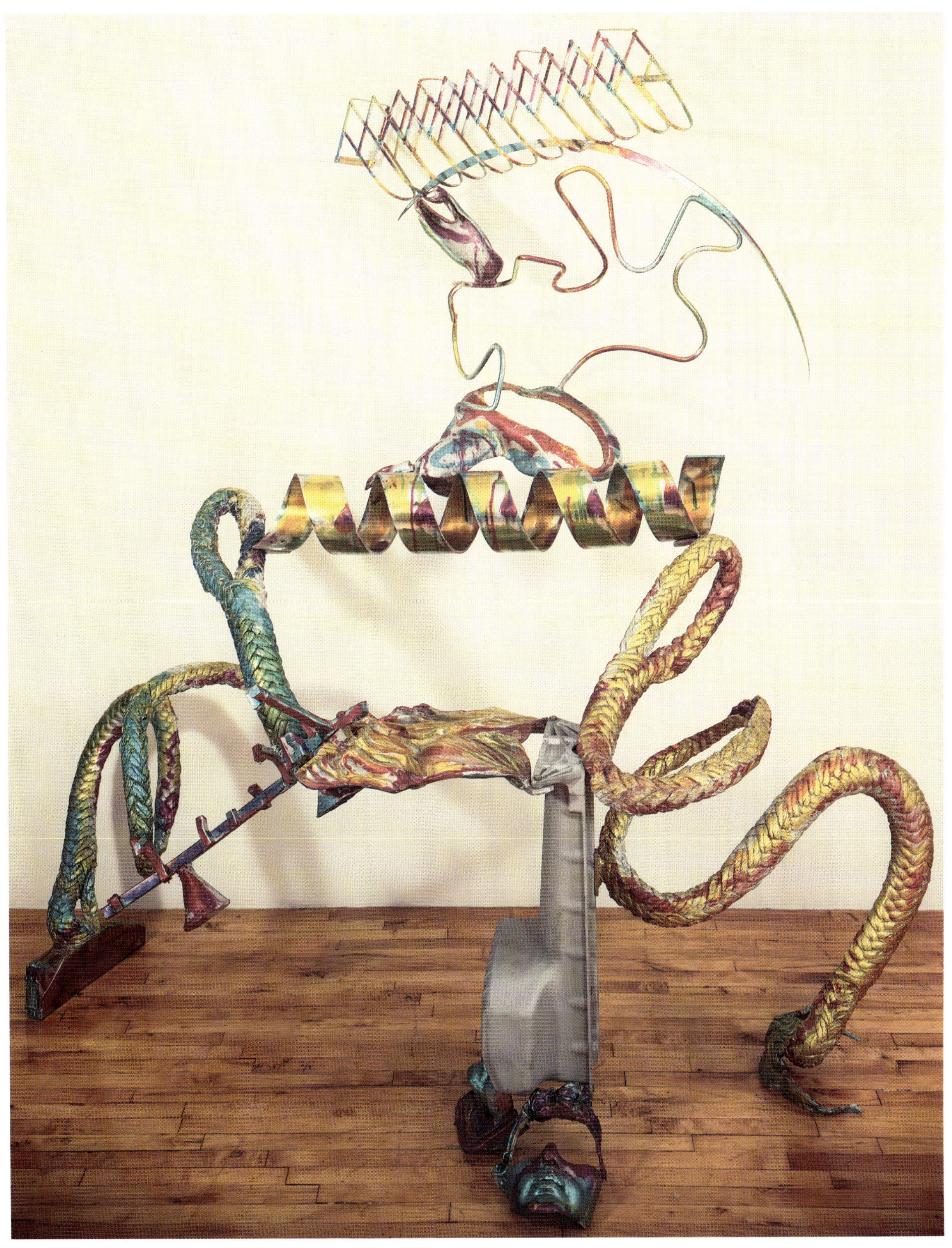

Esthetic Dominance
1989

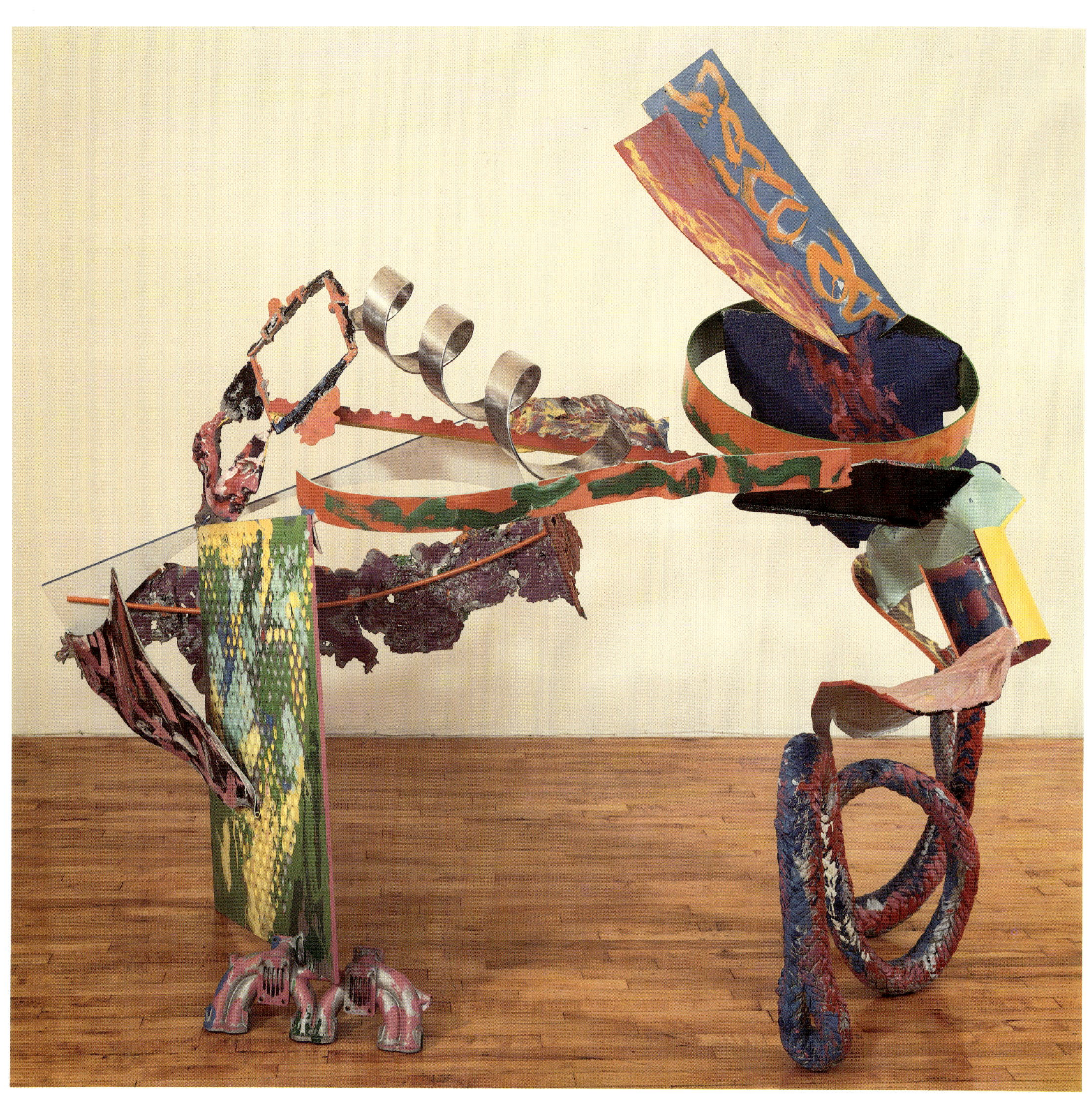

Splendid Mental Isolation

1989

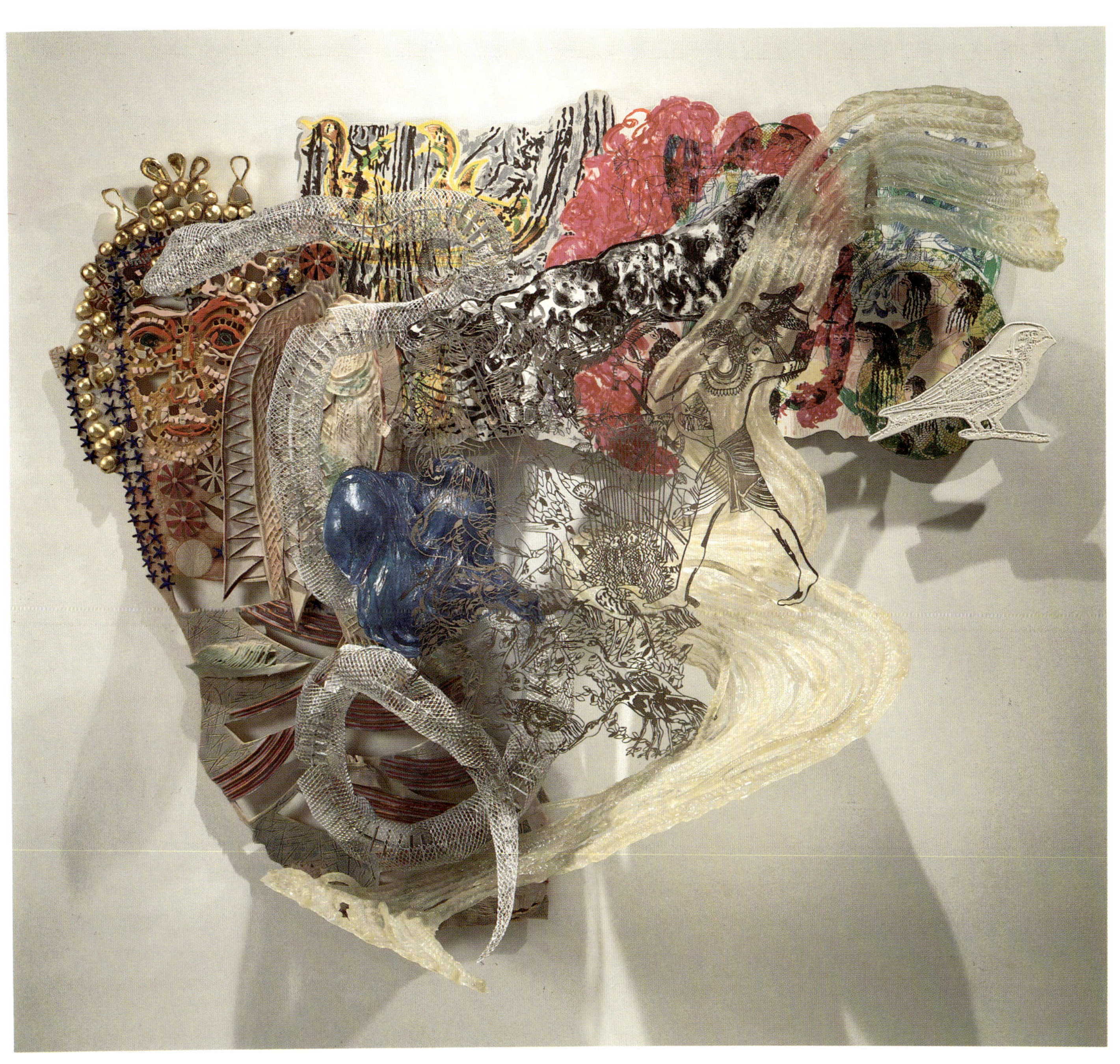

Canoptic Legerdemain

1990

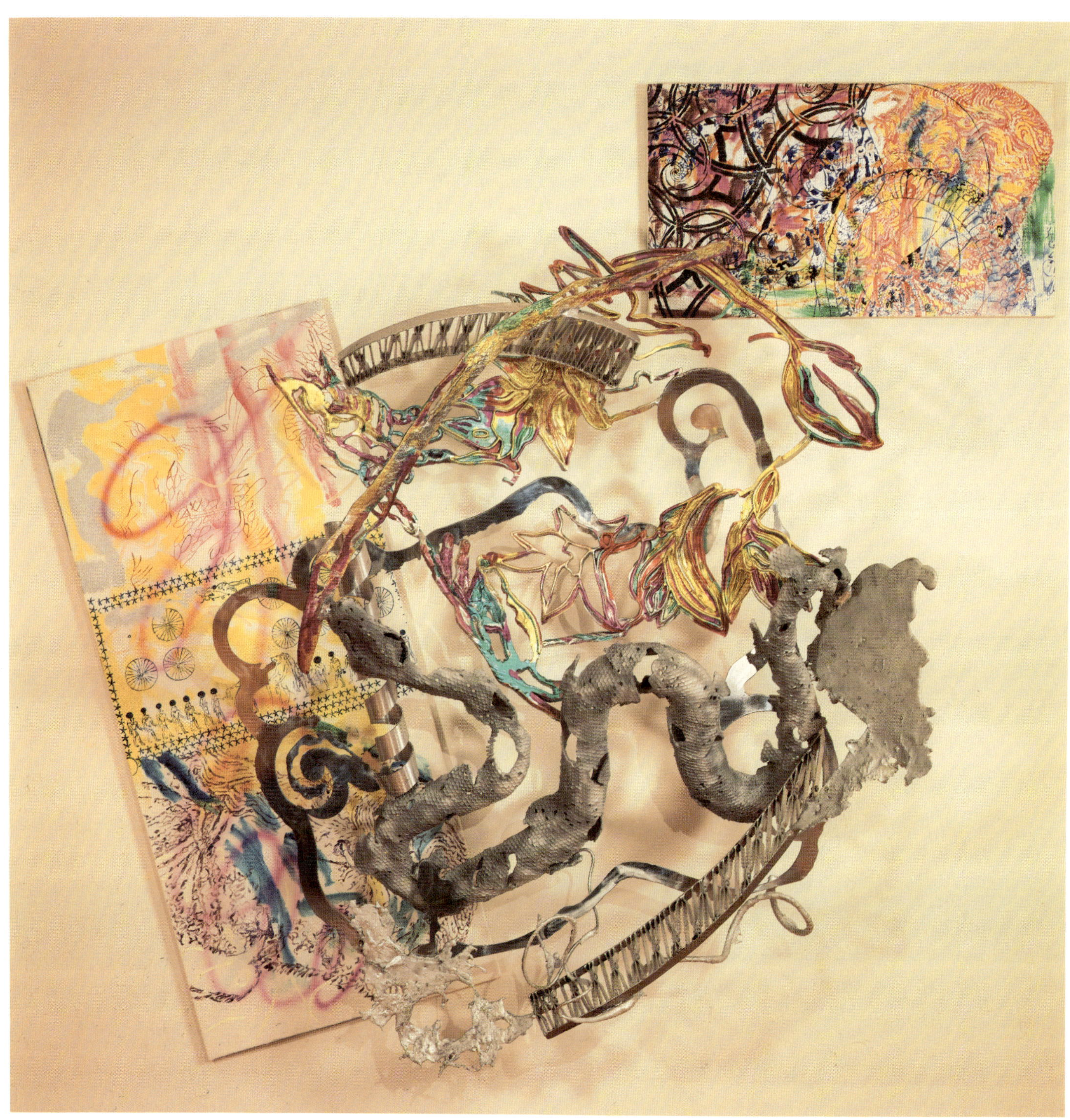

Send Ups of Venerable Traditions
1990

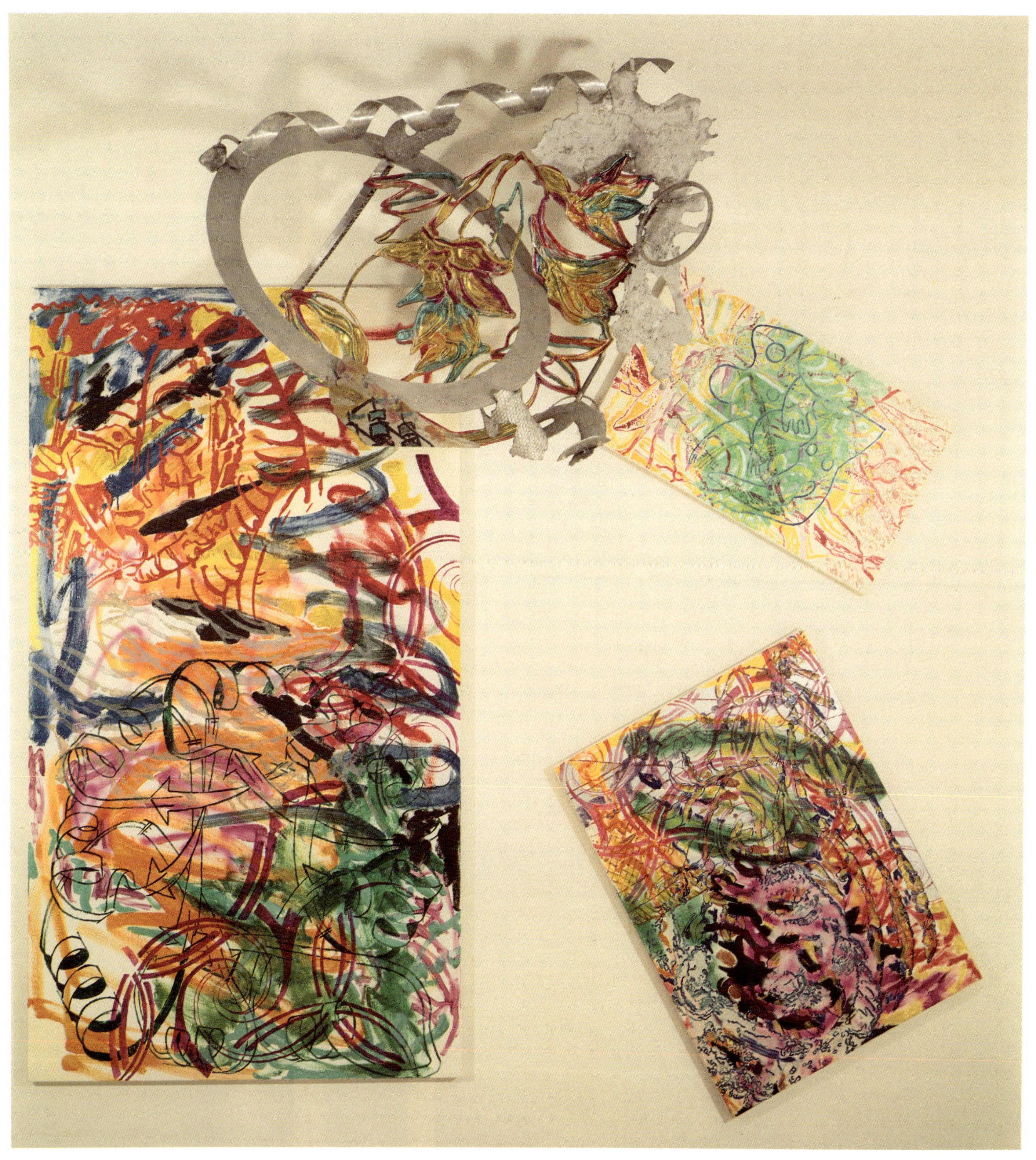

Diagnosing the Canvas
1990–92

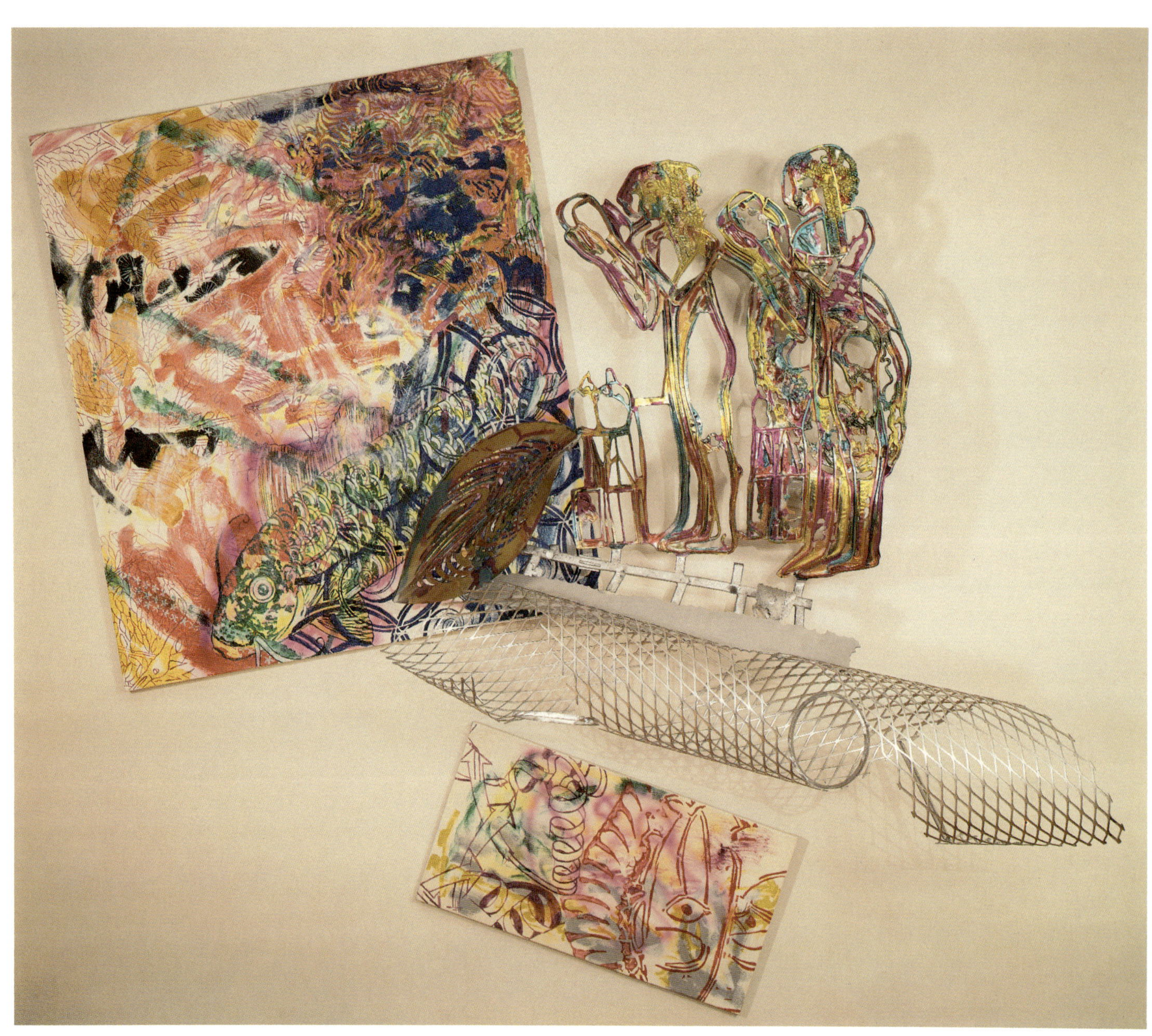

Mutual Implication

1990-92

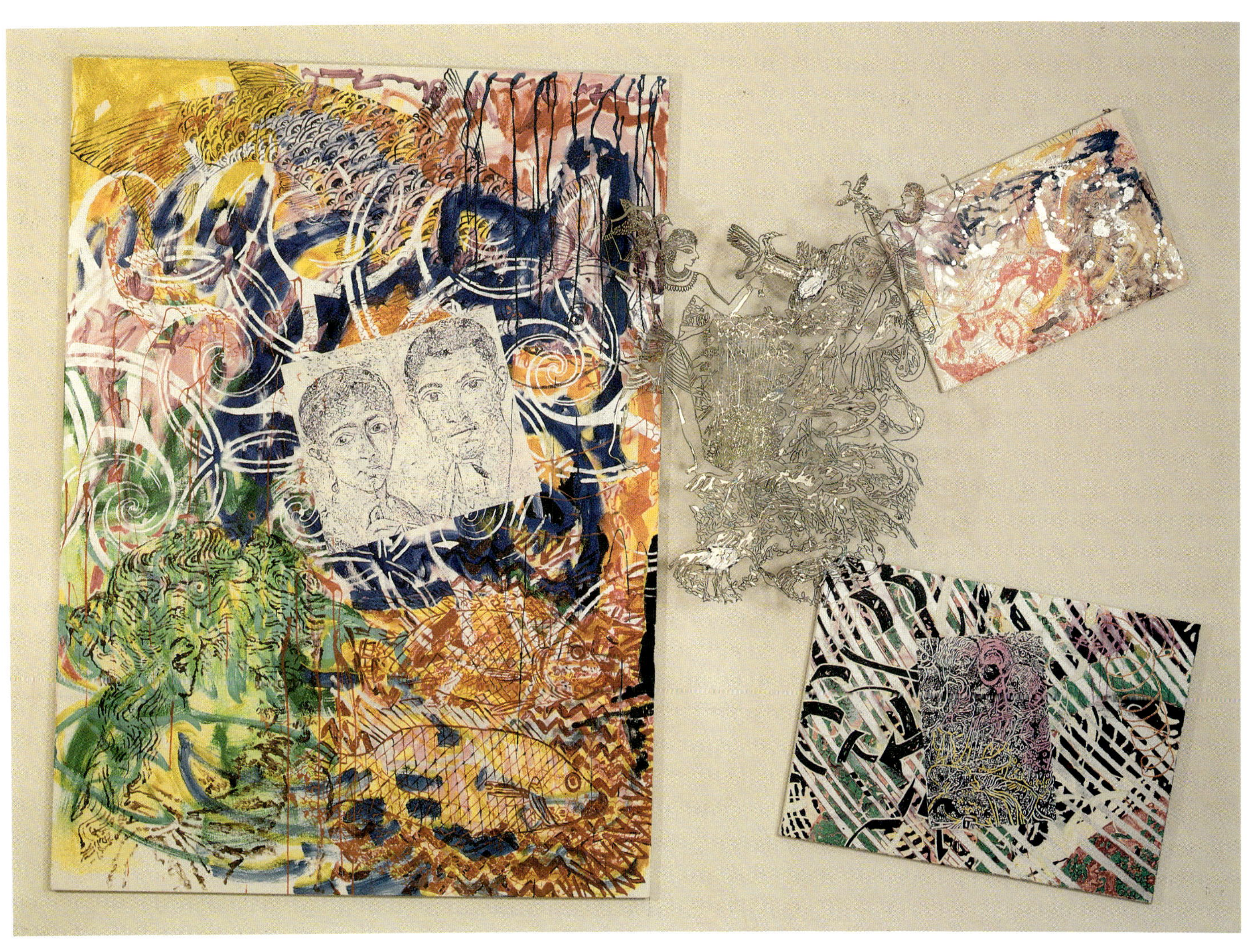

While Embracing
1991

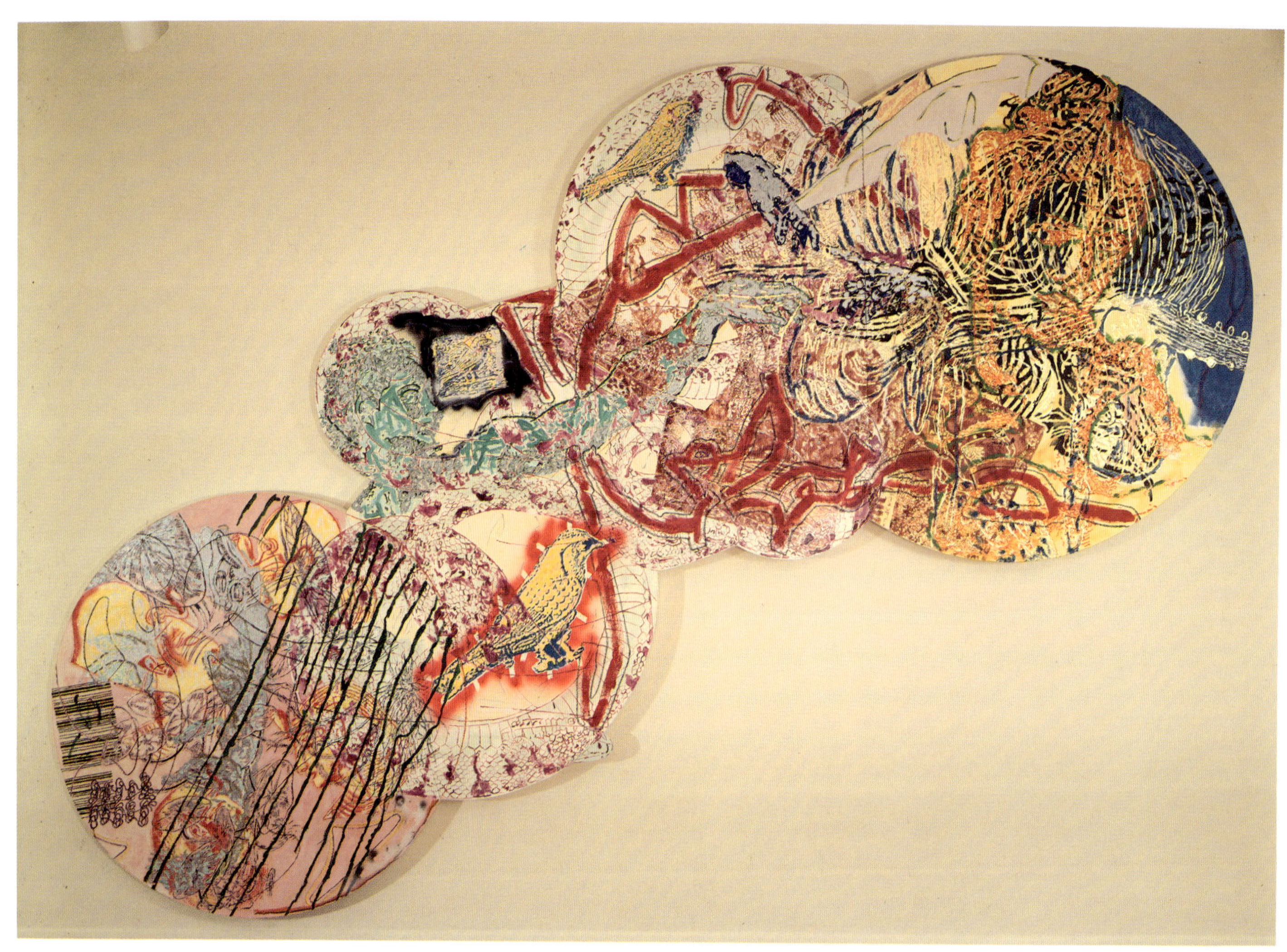

Magnetic Plate of Calls and Answers
1991

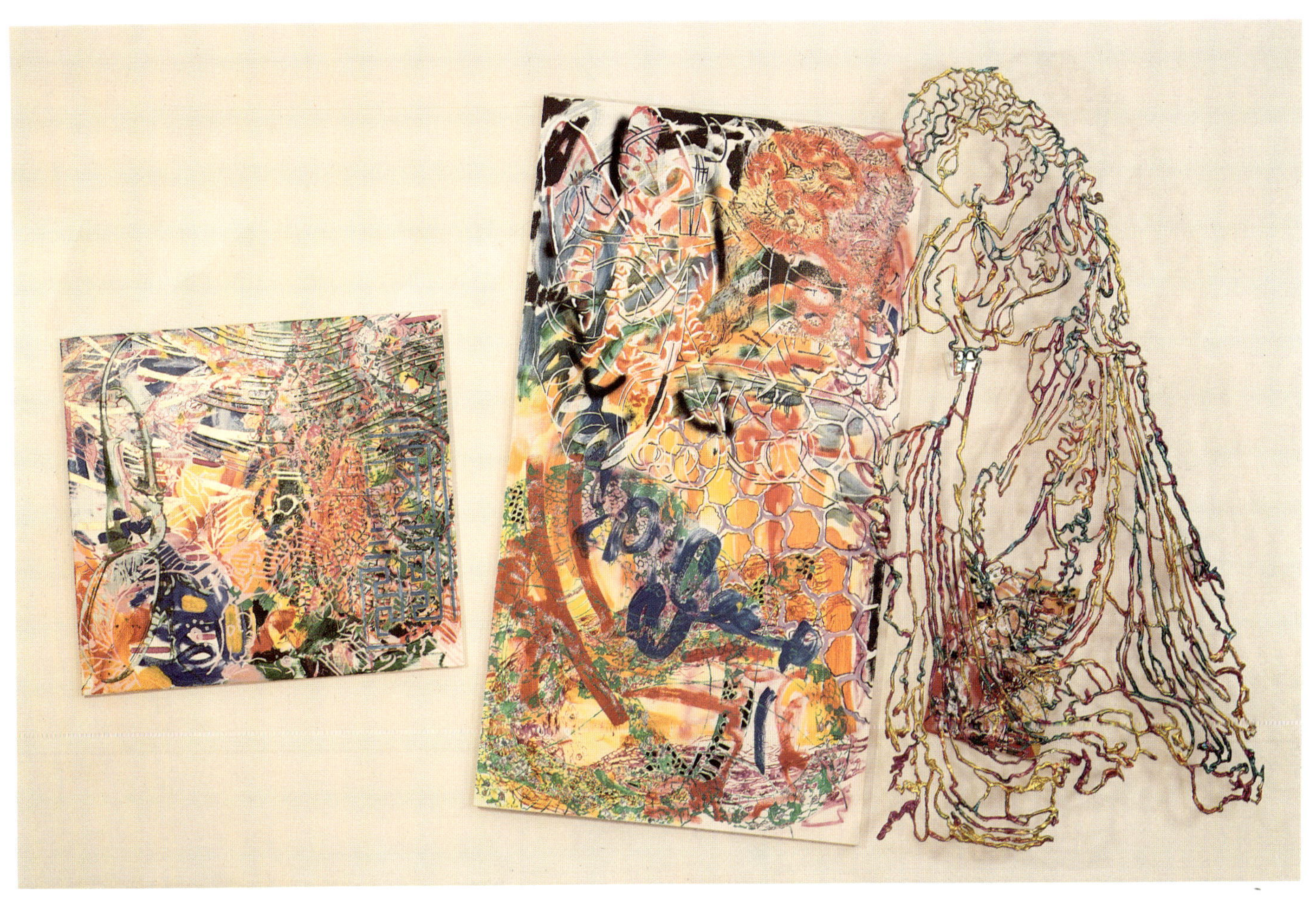

In Care of Solitude
1991

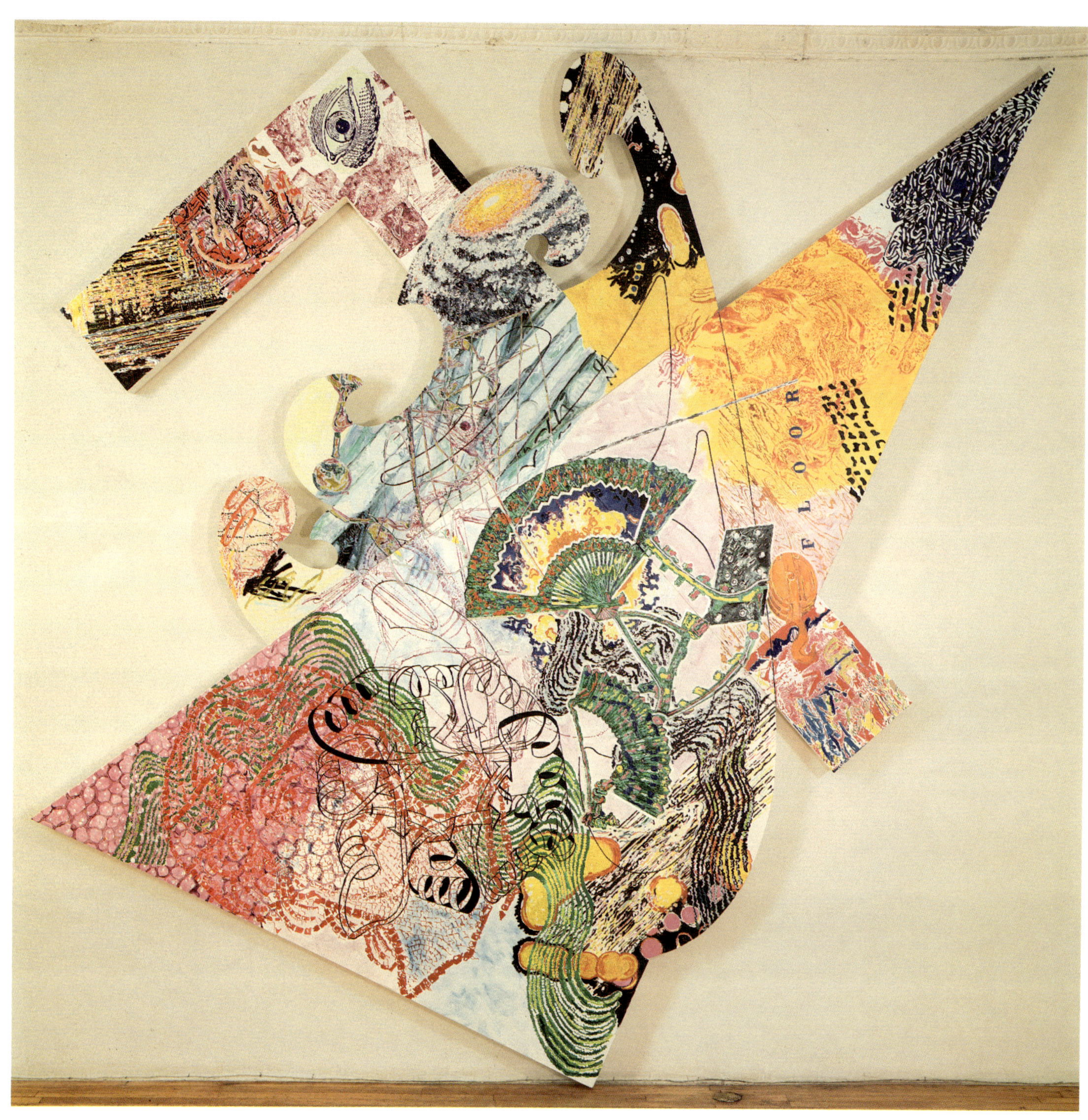

Fat Drops of the Milk of Silence

1991

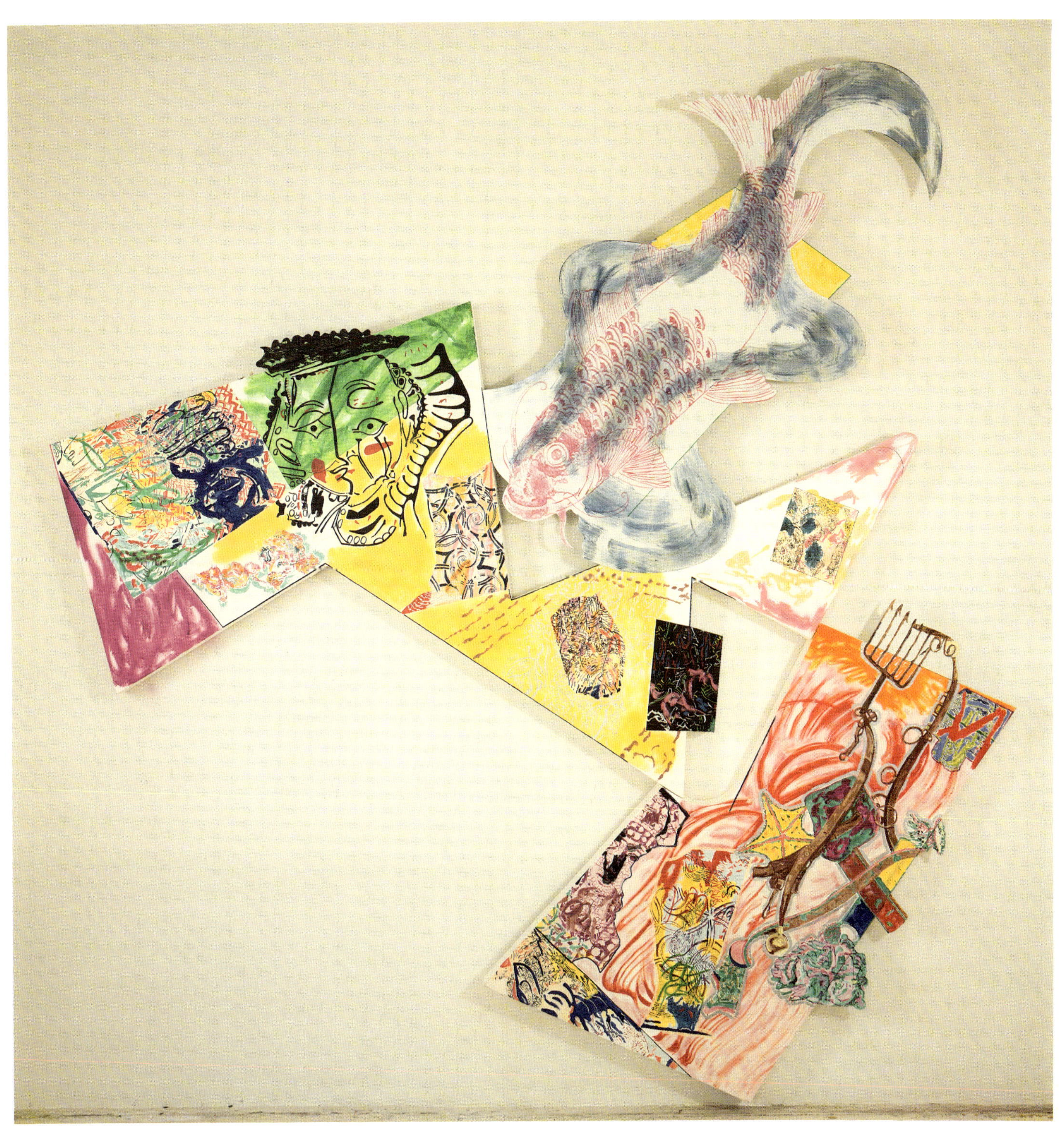

Fish Sleep Entangled in the Hair of the Milky Way
1991

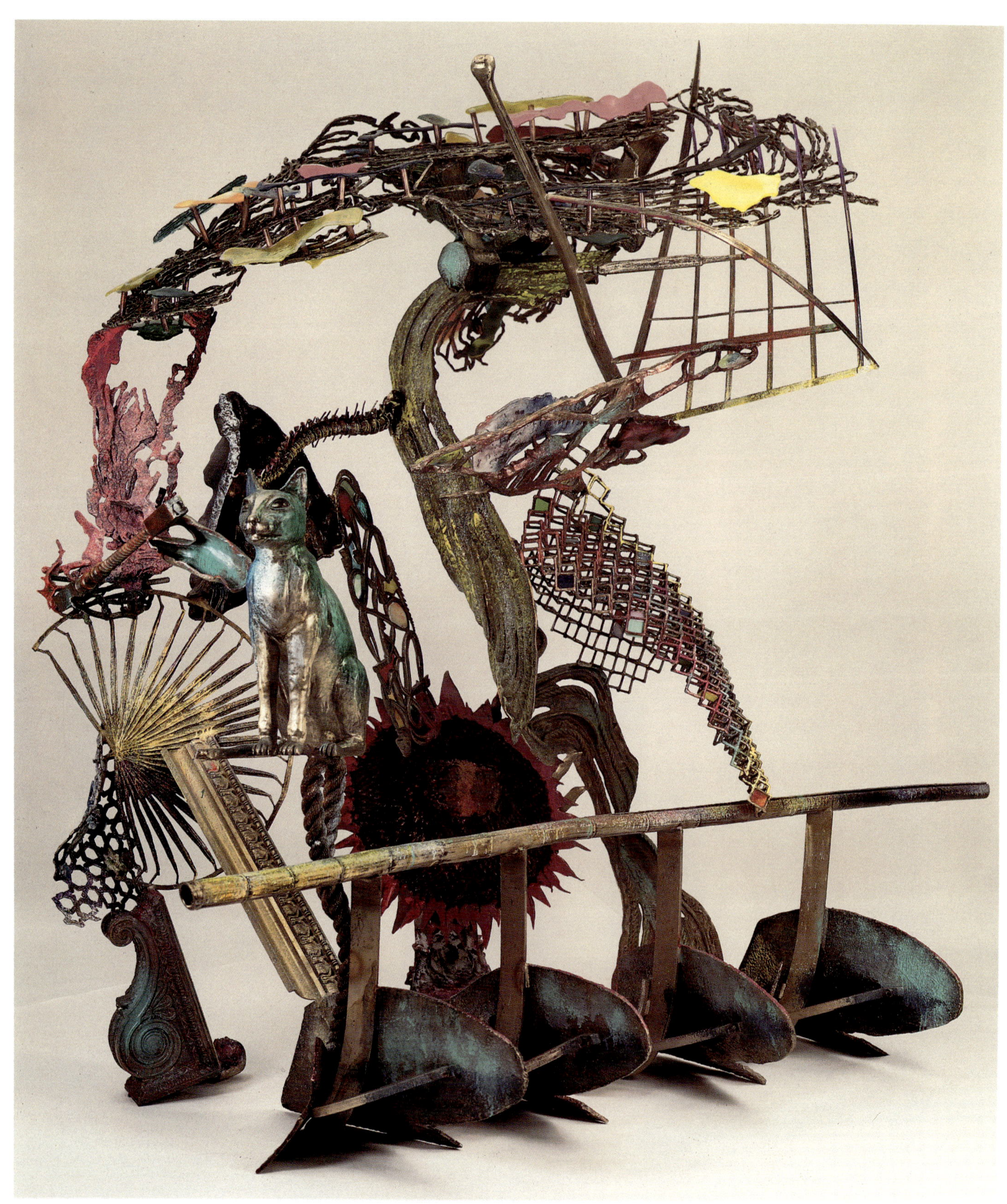

Between Sign and Symbol
1992

Nancy Graves: Translucency

Robert C. Morgan

When Marinetti wrote his Futurist Manifesto in 1909, he espoused that " a roaring car that seems to ride on grapeshot . . . is more beautiful than the Victory of Samothrace." What strikes the reader about this imagery is the violence of its opposition—the conflict of the past in relation to the avant garde culture at the outset of this century.

Her sense of the archeological is of being in the present while excavating the layering of historical evidence, the traces of images from other cultures in other times and in other places in the world.

I allude to this situation at the beginning of Modernism in order to suggest something about the recent sculpture of Nancy Graves. In one sense, Graves is unwittingly engaged with a certain aspect of the Futurist legacy, where the past is disseminated in relation to the present. As we approach the end of the millennium, and presumably the end of the century of Modernism, Nancy Graves has emerged as an artist whose archeological sensibility offers us a new record of the present in relation to the past. She is not beholden to the machine age, as was Marinetti, but she is endowed with the reality of her own age—the information age. Her sense of the archeological is of being in the present while excavating the layering of historical evidence, the traces of images from other cultures in other times and in other places in the world. A recent wall ensemble, *While Embracing* (1991), for example, combines images from ancient Egypt and Greece, erotic images and secular images, signs of opposition and conflict, Eros and Thanatos.

Nancy Graves has been dealing with the problem of sculptural composition for more than two decades. By sculptural composition, I am referring to the notion that space in Graves's sculpture is raw material. To deal with space, the artist has adopted a sense of contour, a way of surrounding space, of capturing space; yet, concomitantly, the artist strives to get inside space in order to reevaluate what is given as virtual reality. According to Gombrich, space offers a sense of identity, a cultural location for the self. What gives Graves's work its presence is the tactility of this idea, a concept that is not merely in suspension, but one that is grounded in the reality of understanding space, her own spatial vocabulary.

Whether a flat ensemble of diagonally poised canvases, such as *While Embracing*, a sculptural relief, such as *Canoptic Legerdemain* (1990), or a freestanding three-dimensional bronze, such as *Between Sign and Symbol* (1992), the spatial and tactile resonances are evident. One aspect of her sculpture is the organizing principle. It is a matter of good design—structurally sound design. Design exists as a means of refinement, but also as a way of stating a position. The position does not have to resort to didacticism; and indeed, this is not the approach that Graves utilizes. Graves carries a formal vocabulary that is well grounded. In this sense, she is like a good architect.

She has a formal sense about her work. Yet to have a formal sense does not imply that formalism is somehow the direction of the work.

What distinguishes Graves from other sculptors of her generation who are possessed by formal acuity is that she looks beyond what is self-evident to what is hidden; that is, her concern for spatiality is the result of a clarity of sensibility. Therefore, when Graves appropriates images and fragments from other cultures, times, and places, she is doing so on the basis of a formal/spatial vocabulary. Her sculpture works because the tensions and balances work, but it exists as something more than a formal strategy. With Graves, form is not a mystique, but a curiosity; in fact, a sculptural reality. To have a stable ground does not mean that one is necessarily outside the currency of the postmodern. What enchants the viewer who is sensitive to Graves's work is its poetry.

In *Canoptic Legerdemain*, the poetic connotations are abundant. There are references to ancient Egypt—papyrus plants—and a fragment of Aphrodite from ancient Greece, traditional Japanese motifs and Michelangelo's *Creation of Adam*. It is constructed out of cast fiberglass elements, laser-cut templates, aluminum board, and other materials that are adhered and wired to one another and to the wall. The sculptural engineering of the piece is remarkable. Also, the piece is rather light in weight. This lightness operates as a metaphor for the sculptural process, deployed in the conception and construction of the piece.

Graves is an artist whose foundation was set well before the fashion for appropriation techniques became widespread in the early 1980s. Her use of art historical and multicultural references is not the sole foundation of her work—either in her two-dimensional paintings or in her hybrid reliefs or in her aluminum and bronze sculpture. The deployment of appropriation and quotational devices in her art is a consequence of her continuing search for significance—not through narrative, but through sign and symbol. One could say that her work is poetic, but not narrative. It carries a certain interplay of semiotic elements based on morphological juxtapositions and association. This interplay of quotational elements allows for a resonance through what semiologists call "deep structure." That is, the relationship of the bust of Aphrodite to an Egyptian falcon or the crying head of Laocoön to the head of Empress Theodora at Ravenna is less about conceptual linkages that have been preset or determined through some form of external schemata. Rather, Graves is dealing with these elements as an operable personal vocabulary of signs. As these personal signs begin to formulate a syntax and thereby achieve the status of a visual semantics within the construct of the work, they may assume symbolic meaning or even, what Samuel Beckett once suggested of Proust, autosymbolic meaning. This is to suggest that Graves is constructing her own context isolated from the history and the culture from which she has appropriated various signs. This is not to suggest that she is oblivious or blindly subversive in relation to her manipulation of visual language; rather it asserts a layering of significance upon the formal ground she has already established. Primarily, Graves determines space in relation to form, then sign in relation to symbol. The action is an intuitive one in that it is dependent upon a process orientation.

The foregoing explanation applies directly to her bronze and glass sculpture called *Between Sign and Symbol* (1992). Superficially, this work has a resemblance to her earlier clock sculpture, cast the same year, entitled *Unending Revolution of Venus, Plants, and Pendulum.* While the early piece has a utilitarian (and symbolic) function—in that it functions as a clock—the more recent work is purely visual and without kinetic components. The resemblance, however, is in the morphological association and interplay between the signs. The relationship of natural and constructed forms is apparent in each. There are elements of Greek statuary, farm tools, filigreed evanescences, plants, discs, ropes, tribal-looking relics, Egyptian heads, fish, pedimental decorum, and more. The signs literally spill over beyond the scope of any rational cohesion.

One cannot expect to find rational cohesion in *Between Sign and Symbol.* It is the very absence of the rational that allows the sculptural presence of these forms to unify themselves intentionally within consciousness. This statement suggests a kind of phenomenology of the sign—not unrelated to the perceptual mechanisms noted by Merleau-Ponty. To see *Between Sign and Symbol* is a matter of entering an experience through the work's visual and material properties. By getting into it, one has to accept certain ground rules—and these ground rules are primarily formal. From the formal follows the linguistic notion of appropriation. This notion is basically poststructural. *Between Sign and Symbol* goes beyond the automatic and unquestioned sign value of the elements. Their semiotic connections are within the personal vocabulary of Graves's visual lexicon. The point being that Graves is not merely playing games with history and culture. She is creating an interplay of sign—transforming, through subconscious effort, the automatic references that are attached to these signs. These signs from ancient Greece and Egypt, for example, run amok in Graves's recent work. They represent, in one sense, the birth of Western culture. They carry a certain weight, a burden within consciousness—in this case, the artist trying to alleviate the burden of these signs as they have come to reflect an oppressive view of history.

Graves's entry into the linguistic galaxy of appropriation through visual sign is a display of intense fortitude. It is a form of representation that exceeds the limits of what is assumed in relation to the birth of culture. It suggests a certain repression whereby the artist is attempting to alleviate the flow held in check by the canon of critical acceptance. *Between Sign and Symbol* represents a passageway out of this historical repression, this burden from the past. It represents a moment of transition—the moment in which the historical sign is suddenly transformed into a personal set of symbols or whereby the signs are subsumed by the artist as a new interplay consisting of weightlessness; in essence, an alleviation from the burden of history, a moment of translucency, of ultimate esthetic clarity, in which the past becomes the present, as if the moment held the mirror of completeness and ecstatic delight.

Another central concern in the work of Nancy Graves since 1979 has been the interaction of color with form. One might attribute this concern to several factors. Probably the most significant is the six-year hiatus that Graves took from sculpture in late 1971 in order to concentrate her efforts on painting. She returned to sculpture in 1977 with a work called *Ceridwen, Out of Fossils. Ceridwen* was a commissioned piece, cast in bronze on a Cor-ten steel base. Typical of her interest in interior skeletal forms as simulations of natural history, *Ceridwen* consists of disarticulated bones of a camel as discovered from the Pleistocene period. In 1978, Graves returned to skeletal and other natural biomorphic forms, perhaps less literal than in the earlier period, but only with a delicately subdued concern for color. (An example would be the variety of patinas used in *Quipu* (1978), a series of bronze-cast floor pieces made from thickly coiled segments of rope.)

It would appear by 1978 that Graves was working through a process of trying to bridge the gap between a more explicit use of color as it had appeared in her early pointillist canvases, as in the *Camouflage* series, dating from 1971, and her *Paleontology* series, being sculptural representations borrowed from observations of natural history.

Color, as one critic has pointed out, has been a means by which Graves distinguishes the various parts of a sculpture from one another and, in a paradoxical way, gives her work a greater three-dimensional presence. One might amplify this comment by saying that color lends a pictorial quality to her sculpture so that elements float in relation to one another in what Graves calls "an energized space." There is little doubt that Graves's use of primary enamels and patinas has an extraordinary effect in this regard. The two versions of *Trace,* from 1980 and 1981, are clear examples.

The later version, currently on permanent display at the Los Angeles County Museum of Art, brings the viewer into contact with an imaginative space and symbolic coherence that defies the rather congested terrace on which it has been sited. The aluminum and steel wire mesh, borrowed from maps and notebooks of ancient Rome, provide much of the quotational subject matter found in the uppermost regions of the ascending sculpture. There is an exuberance in these colors and shapes that defies gravity, just as Marcel Duchamp's domain of the bride defies the gravity of the bachelors in his *Large Glass* (1915-23). The painted elements function literally to define the sculptural presence. In that Graves's sculpture since 1979 tends to work toward the suspension of forms rather than toward gravity (the camels, the carcasses, the fossils), the elements tend to be linear or to follow one another in a contoured spatial sequence.

This is also apparent in two recent works from the current show called *Splendid Mental Isolation* (1989) and *Esthetic Dominance* (1989). In each case, the construct follows a linear assemblage of parts in relation to spatial volume. Thus, the pictoriality is set up in relation to the spatial environment, whether interior or exterior. Like all significant form, the spatial counterpart never acts as a given but as something discovered or called into being. In each of these works, the three-dimensional volume is never static. There is a persistent "dynamicism," in Marinetti's term, that recalls the legacy of the quoted artifacts, shards, and fragments from various cultural arenas.

Is Graves playing hierarchical in relation to these multicultural sources? I think not. Rather, I would look for explanation in terms of alleviating the burden of a cultural hegemony. There is nothing about dominance in the volume of these pieces. There is nothing to suggest a hierarchy of one form over another. It is, in fact, the rhythmic flow that achieves significance through the act of perception.

Again, it is the phenomenology of perception that occurs in relation to following the variables and the permutations of the linear construct as a pictorial experience. Color is essential to this rhythmic flow. In many ways, color substitutes for volume. The lightness of the aluminum implies a reflective surface, a light-sensitive surface; yet the planar elements are always minimized. It is not so much a play of planes as it is of lines. Within the abrupt interstices of the linear flow, one may catch the traces of cultural remains, of fragments of garments, of appendages, signs of ecstasy, of indulgence, of rumination.

There is a certain romantic intrigue about these pieces, an undeniable resistance to the gravity of the past; yet history echoes throughout. The resonance of *Esthetic Dominance*—a wonderful title—gives way to another layering, another circumstance, where meaning is not simply referential, but fully postmodern. This offers a language of signs, but at the same instant, a diffusion of meaning.

To understand these sculptures is a matter of attuning one's vision to their rhythmic flow. It is an esthetic experience—a traditional notion that a special kind of experience exists in relation to the dictum of the eye, a concept borrowed from the Enlightenment. It is a notion that somehow the eye can evoke pleasure, and that pleasure can exist in visual terms. Other critics have spoken eloquently about Graves's equivocation between inspiration and technique—that there is a craftlike elegance both in her sculpture and in her recent painting ensembles such as the remarkable *Magnetic Plate of Calls and Answers* (1991) and *In Care of Solitude* (1991). This artisanry is not simply an indulgence that denies the intention. Rather the artisanry is a means toward achieving an effective palimpsest.

Linguistic philosophers from Umberto Eco to Jacques Derrida have spoken in terms of the palimpsest—the case in which writing occurs over writing—a kind of archeology of signs. Instead of the linear sequencing of signs in terms of grammatical meaning, the palimpsest offers a density, a layering, where meaning retrieves unexpected references from a lost past or a forgotten future—where the sign of writing becomes the writing of the sign. It seems to me that Graves's *Magnetic Plate* is such a work. The visual rhythm of the work is never forsaken, yet within this rhythmic density there is embedded a particular kind of language, a palimpsest. The meaning is sensed through syntactical energy that echoes through the past into the future. The writing never stops, it is continuous. The mystery is never eluded, but is eternally present.

One could speak of the delicacy of the tracery in other works as well. The aluminum-cast ropes that symmetrically bridge *Esthetic Dominance* could be read as snakes—redolent and dynamic, pulsating as they weave an hallucinogenic vision around and between other machine parts. There seems to be a struggle between the refuse of industry and the organic magic of nature that continually intervenes. (Duchamp once made the comment that his *Large Glass* consisted of geometric elements and visceral organs.) The energy is a real factor—the dynamicism. It is no wonder that Calder and David Smith played a fundamental role for Graves in her student years at Yale. The intuitive sense of structure is unmistakable—a structure that seems to reside within the unconscious, one that cannot be a rationalization or predetermined. (Is this why Duchamp gave up working on his *Large Glass*—too much determination?) Yet *Esthetic Dominance* is not simply about mystique. It is evocative of structural parameters that are not readily available in the mundane world. Esthetics are not a part of everyday life in the late twentieth century. This is a fact. For a work of art to evoke feelings that exist beyond the mundane is a considerable feat.

The intuitive structure in *Esthetic Dominance* is a matter of seeing its lightness, of seeing translucency through opacity, of getting the idea through feeling, of sensing the work's wholeness. (Whereas the metaphysics of the past, including Futurism, may have searched for light, the postmodern mode would be more about light*ness*.)

It is a matter of traversing the opaque distance between sign and symbol, as Graves would have it, and of arriving at some inexorable place, some ecstatic insight. The contour drawing is a reasonable prototype for the recent work of Nancy Graves, the drawing in space that knows gravity and yet knows its opposite, its pattern into flight. I am reminded of the early paintings of the Italian Futurists again—Giacomo Balla's study of birds or Severini's interpretation of light—or Boccioni's bronze sculpture, *Unique Forms of Continuity in Space* (1913). I am reminded of the dynamic feeling and lightness inherent in these works. (Marinetti once considered "dynamicism" and "electricism" as alternative names for the movement, but eventually decided on "futurism" as being most expressive of his concept.) Then there are the photographic studies by Muybridge and Marey—the former being an acknowledged source of inspiration for Graves.

Again, there is the emphasis on the kinetic, the mobile, the concept of movement through time and space. Muybridge pursued his concept of human locomotion—through what he called Zoopraxology—in the 1880s and 1890s. Much of his attention was given to the modular seriatim of the human animal—how human bipeds walked, skipped, ran, rode a horse, etc. In spite of Muybridge's scientific authority, there is a passion about these images that is immediately startling and recognizable. This passion—a difficult term to explain, yet somehow innate to some of the greatest accomplishments of our time or any other—may have something to do with the desire to defy gravity. The recognition of gravity as a condition of human life and, formerly, of human history has a certain reality, yet now we have surpassed that assumption. Flight is now as much of a condition as gravity.

For Nancy Graves, these might operate as extended metaphors. The tension between these forces is the tension between the recognition of oppression and opacity in relation to liberation and translucence. The symbolic language of Graves is toward the latter state of mind. Her re-assemblings of historical and cultural fragments are about a celebration of what is possible when the mind is liberated from the hierarchies and oppressions of the past.

Robert C. Morgan is an art critic, artist, and curator who has written extensively on contemporary art in the United States and Europe. He has written catalogues, monographs, and books on a number of artists, including Robert Barry, Marcel Duchamp, and Haim Steinbach.

Conversation with Nancy Graves

David Yager

David Yager: **I would like to begin our discussion in a broad context and work from there. If you could, I'd like you to describe the thought process that allows you to bring these wonderful pieces to reality.**

Nancy Graves: Well, let's talk about the wall pieces. There is *Canoptic Legerdemain* made with Donald Saff and his associates. A lithograph and a lasercut of stainless steel are the two flat wall elements. The others are relief or volumetric, made by fabrication and casting in translucent and light reflective materials. Second, there are the wall pieces comprised of several canvases and a sculpture. Each combines paintings and a sculpture as one unique work. And third, there are the large shaped canvases that contain a depiction in paint of one of my sculptures, among other things. In all of the wall pieces the problem is how to retain specificity while simultaneously bridging from two to three dimensions and vice versa. For me, imagery is metaphor. The specific, recognizable image is made abstract by its function in the piece: how it joins, supports, how its surface incident interfaces compositionally, and finally by its color. Much of the imagery relates to process: shards of fabrication and the casting process become building elements in the sculpture and parallel gesture, which is a structural device in the painting. And there are the organic and scientific forms, historical images from Western civilization as well as the Orient, Africa, and Australia. The images recur, but always to a different purpose. The references are to varied cultures of different time periods, both Western and Oriental, art history, the natural sciences, and acknowledge the increasing availability in the range and depth of information due to technological innovations that daily enhance our grasp of the past as well as future options. In 1987, I titled a work *Clash of Cultures;* another way to say it would be the reverberation of meaning. Essentially, the reverberation of different points of view due to the proximity of cultures that were formerly distant from each other is what we have crashing down on us daily: the clash of economics, social collisions, the clash of history. This is implied in the work through a visual layering.

Yager: **What about the relationship toward the materials that you use, the technology and the culture? You take organic, found objects, and other materials to that next step, your use of new technology, in connection with very old technology. How do these elements and processes interrelate and become part of the process?**

Graves: Process. My work comes out of the sixties, where process was a focal point; it has always been a consideration and the "how" of the making of the piece remains evident in its final form. For example, I have chosen to include aspects of the casting process such as gating material, sprews, crucibles, the encasement of the crucible, and bronze and aluminum spillovers. The casting process, which dates to China around 3000 B.C., contrasts with the laser cut on steel, which is pretty much state of the art, or bright hued anodized aluminum. Paints developed for outdoor usage in the eighties are constantly being amended. Surfaces are painterly. Recently I have been casting, slumping, fusing, and working in off hand glass to be combined with bronze. Process is evident here also.

YAGER: AS YOU START TO INCORPORATE YOUR PAINTINGS WITH THE WALL SCULPTURE, WHICH HAS A VERY DIFFERENT TRADITION AND A DIFFERENT WAY OF WORKING AND VIEWING, HOW DO YOU THINK ABOUT THE PIECES IN TERMS OF MAKING THAT TRANSITION AND INCORPORATING THEM SO THEY DON'T BECOME TWO SEPARATE PIECES, BUT EXIST AS ONE?

GRAVES: Well that, of course, is the fun of it. The challenge is first of all to develop a visual dialogue between the canvas surface and the wall sculpture through placement, color, line, gesture, and image. In each of the canvas parts I've tried to create a different visual statement through its graphic color, quality, the coloration, the type of imagery, the scale, depth of space, use of spray paint versus brushing, varied techniques that integrate with the whole: and create a lyric balance of imbalance, causing the eye to move from three to two dimensions and back again.

YAGER: COULD YOU EXPAND A LITTLE ON TWO AREAS: THE OBJECTS, YOU CALL PARTS, AND THE INVENTORY OF YOUR PARTS AND HOW YOU WORK IN TERMS OF SELECTION AND INVENTORY OF THOSE PARTS AS YOU START BUILDING YOUR PIECES, AND SOMETHING WE TOUCHED ON AT ANOTHER TIME, THE CONTEXT OF THE FORMS OF THOSE PIECES?

GRAVES: Well, I've been working in direct assembly with an inventory of up to a thousand cast or fabricated forms, except for large commissions. Just as one has paint in a tube, I have available pieces in aluminum and bronze of different sizes, dimensions, rhythms, spatial functions, and building options depending on the nature of the given sculpture or relief. What distinguishes these pieces is that each form, each cast or fabricated part, functions foremost as a building element in the finished piece. The original meaning of any part is subsumed in its placement and function, albeit its meanings are more repercussive, more layered, as the range of eclectic forms, art historical from diverse cultures and categories has increased. More recently, I've been working on outdoor pieces that combine large sections of previous sculptures. I made models even though these are not excessively large (about ten to eleven feet tall) because of their complexity. For engineering purposes I investigate further the function of each of the parts relative to a specific piece prior to its casting. In each case the possibility of creating has different options, which is a limitation but also an opening.

YAGER: IN THE SELECTION OF OBJECTS, WHY DO CERTAIN OBJECTS BECOME NANCY GRAVES SYMBOLS? WHAT CAUSES CERTAIN OBJECTS TO

HAVE AN AFFINITY TO YOU, THAT YOU DECIDE TO TAKE OUT OF CONTEXT, CAST, AND BRING BACK AS SOMETHING VERY DIFFERENT, SOMETIMES VERY RECOGNIZABLE BUT IN ITS NEW CONTEXT VERY DIFFERENT?

GRAVES: Well, to address specifically what's in these relief pieces, there are fabricated elements, there are spillovers and gating elements, there are figurative forms. There are parts of Hellenistic sculptures: heads, arms, feet, hands. I cut in half the head of the Venus de Milo to test the extent of visual recognition through its fragmentation. And why did I choose these forms? Because Hellenistic sculptures are cultural metaphors representing the beginning of Western sculpture. They are icons in their own right, which then can be integrated without giving up their identity but yielding to the larger whole. Additional elements could be a rope, which through its configuration has the connotation of a snake, such as in the large anodized aluminum sculpture. I have selected organic material, plants, plant forms, sardines for their rhythm and their non-sculptural origin.

YAGER: I STARTED TO THINK ABOUT SOME OF THESE PIECES AS VIGNETTES IN A FILM OR FRAMES IN A FILM, OR AS IF SOMETHING IS ABOUT TO HAPPEN, AND THEY START TO TAKE ON MUCH MORE OF A TIME BASE SENSE THAN I HAD EXPERIENCED BEFORE. I WONDER IF THAT IS AN IMPORTANT ELEMENT; IS THAT SOMETHING YOU'VE EVER CONSIDERED RELATIVE TO THESE PIECES?

GRAVES: You mean that they are anticipatory suspended motion, that they seem to be about to become something?

YAGER: YES. THAT THERE'S A FEELING OF A WEIGHT, MOVING DOWN OR FALLING. THERE'S A SENSE OF TIME, NOT IN THE LITERAL SENSE OF A NARRATIVE, BUT MUCH MORE IN A SPIRITUAL SENSE.

GRAVES: They're motile, the illusion of motion, the act of becoming. And that reading depends on, which is true in two- or three-dimensional work, one's relationship to the forms and, obviously with sculpture, particularly large ones, there's much more possibility to move around it. So that the final summation would be a mental composite varied according to the viewer and the viewing, which does relate to film. In making films I thought about this a great deal. The linear narrative time element relates to a certain extent to the printmaking process. Visual overlay or image layering in two dimensions parallels the out-of-context juxtapositions of parts which analogize as chapters to a novel.

YAGER: WHEN YOU TALK ABOUT LAYERS, I WAS THINKING ABOUT THEM IN TERMS OF MULTIPLE LAYERS IN FILM. IN YOUR NEW PIECES, ESPECIALLY WHAT IS TRANSPARENT, YOU'RE BLOCKED OUT, YOU'RE MASKED OUT OF OTHER THINGS AND THAT'S MAYBE WHERE THAT CINEMATIC TIME BASE SENSE I'M TALKING ABOUT HAPPENS.

GRAVES: Then time is your perception of it in this case rather than its motion, which is mechanical.

YAGER: RIGHT. IT BECOMES MUCH MORE OF AN EMOTIONAL ELEMENT OF TIME RATHER THAN ANYTHING ELSE.

GRAVES: And its "meaning" would be closer to poetry than to prose.

YAGER: YES. I START TO THINK ABOUT IT IN TERMS OF FILM OR DANCE, WHERE YOU HAVE ONE PERSON PERFORMING ACROSS THE STAGE AND SIX OTHER THINGS HAPPENING BEHIND THEM, INCLUDING LAYERS OF SCENERY AND SO FORTH.

GRAVES: So the perception is orchestrated in a sense. Disparate readings can occur in any given piece and recognition of the whole is dependent upon the way in which the encounter occurred. And just as the meaning in rereading a novel can never be the same twice, the reexperiencing of a dance is always unique. I read Anton Ehrenzweig early on when making the camels and developed an attitude about perception that concurred with his ideas: namely, that viewing becomes cumulative and is an empirical digestion and internalization of the object that is unique to every individual. No two people will ever hear the same Beethoven sonata in the same way. This caused me to think of variability, repetition, fragmentation, serialization in sculpture and led to sculptures that display a kind of motility in three dimensions, a stasis depending on where the eye focuses.

YAGER: A QUESTION THAT ALWAYS SEEMS TO BE ASKED OF ARTISTS, CERTAINLY IN THE CONTEXT OF UNIVERSITIES AND STUDENTS, BUT I THINK OF ANYONE WHO IS A SERIOUS COLLECTOR, A SERIOUS VIEWER, IS THE WAY THE ARTIST THINKS ABOUT THINGS, THINKS ABOUT THE PROCESS AND WORKS THROUGH TO THE FINAL FINISHED PIECE. COULD YOU WALK US THROUGH YOUR METHOD YOU MIGHT USE IN CONSTRUCTING ONE OF THE PIECES OF SCULPTURE, WHETHER YOU WORK FROM DRAWINGS, WHETHER YOU WORK FROM SMALL SCALE MODELS? PLEASE GIVE US A SENSE OF HOW THE PIECES COME ALIVE.

GRAVES: Generally, I don't work from sketches unless it's an outdoor sculpture where one needs an engineer and therefore has to know early on what the configurations will be. What I rely on is intuition and past experience. Often I think in terms of trying an idea related to a recent sculpture problem up to three times. So let's say I'm going to make a sculpture of maybe ten feet tall. There are structural considerations as to how the piece is going to touch the ground, the weight displacement, and the overall gesture of the sculpture. If it's a direct assembly, I will be checking out the inventory as I work with the welders and whomever it is assisting with the crane. Once the piece gets underway I find forms faster than I can think, but it's a kind of empirical knowing. If I have this snake form, for example, I can intellectualize it as a spiral armature. It's a large element, high in surface incident, for example, but a timeless repetitive form. It's not uniquely varied as, by contrast, a plant would be for example, where the flower and the leaf are discrete parts. It would *lend* itself to the sculpture. It's not crying out for attention in terms of its own identity. And I would probably start to build the middle section, not with the idea that it might ultimately end up as the middle part but that it could move either down or up. The middle section can become a base or the top. Also if it's large, it has to be taken apart as I'm building. I discuss how it will come apart with the welders and whomever is in charge of doing that type of work subsequently. And so let's say I lay out pieces on the floor for A, B, and C and start to weld them. And then maybe once I had put together most of the parts for the B section, I would hold it up with the crane and at the same time work with the top layer (C) and juxtapose them. Of course what I have to discuss is the balance of imbalance. How can these forms support each other and how can I push it to the limit in terms of its structural tension. And at a certain point I'll have all the general concepts and building blocks laid out and integrated into the piece, and then I'll probably stop and give the men time to hard weld the piece, because when you assemble that fast it's just tack welding, which can get to be dangerous. It does allow me to make changes, and I might come back another day and then find I want to change the individual parts. Occasionally I remove something because either it's not strong enough, or we might discover along the way that there were flaws in the casting, or it might be a form of a different metal and there might be some problems in the welding. But generally my decisions are firm, and then I add forms that will enhance the piece structurally once there's been time to determine that it's a little weak here and what we can do over there so it will come apart. And so we need to put this connection in, and how to disguise that separation, etc., etc.

YAGER: IN PUTTING THE PIECES TOGETHER DO YOU FIND AS YOU LOOK AT AN OBJECT IT COMES TOGETHER, OR IS IT A PROCESS, VERY THOUGHT OUT AND MECHANICALLY DECIDED? I GUESS I'M CURIOUS ABOUT THE SPIRIT, DO THE PARTS JUST FIT TOGETHER AND THEN YOU STEP BACK AND IT'S CLEAR? IN GATHERING THE MATERIALS AND PUTTING THESE PIECES TOGETHER, COULD YOU TALK ABOUT THE FLOW OR THE MOMENT IN TIME WHEN YOU MAKE YOUR DECISIONS? ABOUT WHICH PIECES FIT WELL WITH WHICH OTHER PIECES?

GRAVES: When I select a form, I do so not primarily for its content but for its anticipated function. The eight sardines that I roped together offer at least sixteen places, tail and head, to weld. They function to join any number of other components and present a varied, repetitive rhythm. The belly of the Venus de Milo, how do I think of it? Ten per cent for its history, ninety per cent for its form, for its configuration, its mass, its strength, and how many points in space, how many ways it can be joined or welded. The sardines roped together act like a spine or an armature that moves from top to bottom on a diagonal and integrates all the elements. In *Canoptic Legerdemain*, the print on the top contrasts with the laser cut, with the epoxy cast of the Aphrodite from the Elgin marbles to the snake, and in the Theodora and the wave in the lower left, which is the largest element in the piece as well. Each has a unique linear pattern. Size is another factor. Something small can't join that much but can be a stabilizer. Geometric elements oppose organic forms, fabricated forms of sheet metal contrast a rhythm in a particular place. Forms whose functions and configurations are dissimilar can be visually related. The parallel spikes of a palmetto leaf are the equivalent of a rope of parallel sardines, for example, and thereby strengthen the visual reading of the piece.

YAGER: SO IN FACT YOU'RE THINKING SOMETIMES TWO-DIMENSIONALLY AND THEN LATER THREE-DIMENSIONALLY BECAUSE OF THE KINDS OF OBJECTS AND SURFACES YOU'RE WORKING WITH SIMULTANEOUSLY IN TRYING TO READ THOSE OBJECTS FROM MULTIPLE DISTANCES AND DIFFERENT POINTS AS THEY'RE ASSEMBLED.

Graves: Absolutely. And I'm also drawing on the discrete histories of these forms, my anticipation of what they're becoming in the immediate sculpture, how they have been used in previous work.

Yager: Yet, its clear that the processes are really additive, building processes you have worked with over a number of years. An understanding of what went before very clearly builds on that process of how you use materials, taking more risks as the materials become more comfortable and pushing them into new directions.

Graves: Yes. Direct assembly as additive process is the overall concern of creating tension between imbalance through counterbalance of open non-massive groupings, and it parallels with stasis and motility at the same time. This is further emphasized by repetition of various forms, by placement of particular shapes and textures, by rhythms within the sculpture, choices of content, etc.

Yager: Is there an internal voice that moves you along or speaks to you when you're working or an internal dialogue that takes place with yourself?

Graves: There's a reliance on the intuitive and a confidence in knowing that I have done X, Y, and Z in the past so I can attempt to jump in the stream, so to speak, to reach beyond this and let things happen and take advantage of them as they occur. If, for example, when I'm building, something comes out other than anticipated, I will take that awareness and integrate it into the piece rather than destroy it, which further emphasizes the directness of the assembly, the option for growth as the piece evolves. I might use that unexpected result as the theme for, let's say, three or four pieces in the future. That's the exciting aspect of working. Occasionally, an assistant will suggest something by the way he stands and holds something or the fact that he might be next to a piece and, without wanting to, say, well, why don't you use this kind of thing. I key into their experience and understanding of what I'm about as they participate in the making of the sculpture.

Yager: From my standpoint, this has been a fantastic experience for me knowing your work earlier, but having the advantage now of spending more time with the work and doing a number of interviews with you, its given me many insights not only into your work but into the way I think about other things beyond just looking at the work. What I keep coming back to is this sense of your confidence, which allows you to take bigger risks as you look at new materials, and that includes aspirations built on all kinds of what I sometimes call baggage, or what you brought along with you, or that encyclopedia of knowledge, or whatever that information is. The new work really shows that. I'm thrilled, and I can't wait to get it all up and look at it.

Graves: Well, I would like to thank you for those thoughts and also to explain your effect on the work. Our conversation elicits thoughts allowing me to move into other areas as well and to see things in the work anew. So this has been a very interesting and very pleasant experience.

Checklist of the Exhibition

All dimensions are in inches;
height precedes width precedes depth.

1. **Esthetic Dominance**
   1989
   Anodized aluminum
   85 1/2 x 84 x 56
   Courtesy of Knoedler & Co., New York

2. **Splendid Mental Isolation**
   1989
   Aluminum with polyurethane paint
   81 1/2 x 100 x 57 1/2
   Courtesy of Knoedler & Co., New York

3. **Canoptic Legerdemain**
   1990
   Color lithograph mounted on aluminum, stainless steel, resin, painted casts from epoxy, sand, marble dust
   78 1/2 x 95 x 35
   Courtesy of the Artist
   On loan to the Fine Arts Gallery, U.M.B.C., only

4. **Send Ups of Venerable Traditions**
   1990
   Oil on canvas, anodized aluminum
   77 1/4 x 92 1/2 x 24, overall
   left: 20 x 36, anodized aluminum: 65 x 58 x 24,
   right: 60 x 27
   Courtesy of Knoedler & Co., New York

5. **Diagnosing the Canvas**
   1990-92
   Oil on canvas, anodized aluminum
   104 x 100 x 33 1/2, overall
   left: 80 x 45, anodized aluminum: 54 x 51 x 33 1/2
   top right: 20 x 34,
   lower right: 40 x 30
   Courtesy of Knoedler & Co., New York

6. **Mutual Implication**
   1990-92
   Oil on canvas, anodized aluminum
   102 x 107 x 36, overall
   left: 60 x 54, anodized aluminum: 72 x 77 x 36,
   right: 20 x 38
   Courtesy of Knoedler & Co., New York

7. **While Embracing**
   1991
   Oil on canvas, stainless steel, and acrylic
   86 x 125 x 8 1/4, overall
   left: 86 x 64, stainless steel laser cut: 45 x 41 1/2 x 8 1/4
   right top: 20 x 30,
   lower right: 30 x 42
   Courtesy of Knoedler & Co., New York

8. **Magnetic Plate of Calls and Answers**
   1991
   Oil, gold leaf on canvas, and alucobond
   109 x 190
   Courtesy of Knoedler & Co., New York

9. **In Care of Solitude**
   1991
   Oil, gold leaf, glitter on canvas, and aluminum
   85 x 138 x 9 1/2, overall
   left: 40 x 44, center: 80 x 45,
   right: 20 x 14
   anodized aluminum: 85 x 45 x 9 1/2
   Courtesy of Knoedler & Co., New York

10. **Fat Drops of the Milk of Silence**
    1991
    Acrylic, oil, white gold leaf on canvas, and alucobond
    125 1/2 x 123
    Courtesy of Knoedler & Co., New York

11. **Fish Sleep Entangled in the Hair of the Milky Way**
    1991
    Oil, acrylic, white gold leaf on canvas, and alucobond
    105 x 102
    Courtesy of Knoedler & Co., New York

12. **Between Sign and Symbol**
    1992
    Bronze with polychrome patina, slumped and fused glass
    108 x 112 x 80
    Courtesy of the Artist
    On loan to the Fine Arts Gallery, U.M.B.C., only

Recent Exhibitions & Bibliography

Solo

1989

Nancy Graves: New Sculpture, Knoedler Kasmin Gallery, London, England, April 4 - May 3, 1989.

Nancy Graves: New Work, Knoedler & Company, New York, NY, October 7 - 28, 1989.

Nancy Graves, Linda Cathcart Gallery, Santa Monica, CA, November 11 - December 9, 1989.

1990

Nancy Graves, the Clash of Cultures: New Paintings on Paper and Sculpture, Gerald Peters Gallery, Santa Fe, NM, July 3 - 21, 1990; Gerald Peters Gallery, Dallas,TX, September 24 - October 24, 1990.

Nancy Graves, Heland Wetterling Gallery, Gothenburg, Sweden, October 6 - November 7, 1990. Catalogue.

1991

Nancy Graves; Paradigm and Paradox, Marion Locks Gallery, Philadelphia, PA, March 12 - April 27, 1991. Catalogue.

Energy Fields Transfixed: Recent Works by Nancy Graves, Meredith Long & Company, Houston, TX, April 11 - 30, 1991.

Skin Series, Knoedler & Company, New York, NY, October 5 - 31, 1991.

1992

Alchemy of Time, Irving Galleries, Palm Beach, FL, February 11 - March 3, 1992.

Group

1989

Art of Lasting Value, Consistency & Change, Gallery Camino Real, Boca Raton, FL, February 10 - March 3, 1989.

Sculpture 1960s - 1980s, The Greenberg Gallery, St. Louis, MO, March 4 - April 22, 1989.

Lines of Vision: Drawings by Contemporary Women, Hillwood Art Gallery, Long Island University, Brookville, NY, May 12 - June 28, 1989. Curated by Judy Van Wagner. Book of same name published by Hudson Hills Press, NY.

Making Their Mark: Women Artists Move Into the Mainstream, 1970-85, Cincinnati Art Museum, February 22 - April 2, 1989; New Orleans Museum of Art, May 6 - June 18, 1989; Denver Art Museum, July 22 - September 10, 1989; Pennsylvania Academy of Fine Arts, October 20 - December 31, 1989. Book published by Abbeville Press.

Land, Sea, Air, Steven Scott Gallery, Baltimore, MD, April 4 - 29, 1989.

First Impressions, Walker Art Center, Minneapolis, MN, June 4 - September 10, 1989. Catalogue.

Ken Tyler - 25 Glorious Years, Heland Wetterling Gallery, Stockholm, Sweden, May 24 - August 13, 1989. Catalogue.

Public Art Program, Hillwood Gallery, Long Island University, Brookville, NY, C.W. Post Campus, May 24 - August 13, 1989. Catalogue.

Important Works on Paper, Meredith Long & Company, Houston, TX, September 12 - October 20, 1989. Catalogue, ill. p. 13.

The Development of Sculptural Form, Associated American Artists, New York, December 5 - 30, 1989. Catalogue, ill. nos. 35 - 45.

The Experience of Landscape, Whitney Museum of American Arts Downtown at Federal Reserve Plaza, New York, December 12, 1989 - March 2, 1990. Catalogue.

The New American Landscape: Selections from the Museum Collection, The Museum of Fine Arts, Houston, TX.

Recent Acquisitions: Works by Women in the Pennsylvania Academy's Collection, Philadelphia, PA, November 17 - December 31, 1989.

1990

Heland Wetterling Gallery Shows Knoedler Gallery Artists, Heland Wetterling Gallery, Stockholm, Sweden, April 7 - 24, 1990. Catalogue.

Newer Sculpture, Charles Cowles Gallery, New York, NY, June 1 - 29, 1990.

New Member Sculptures Exhibition, The Century Club, New York, NY, February 27 - March 30, 1990.

Exhibition of Work by Newly Elected Members and Recipients of Awards, American Academy and Institute of Arts and Letters, New York, NY, May 16 - June 10, 1990.

Color in Art: American Expressions from the Mid - Twentieth Century to the Present, Samuel P. Harn Museum of Art, University of Florida, Gainesville, FL, September 22 - December 2, 1990. Brochure, ill. p. 4.

Painted Forms: Recent Metal Sculpture, Whitney Museum of American Art at Philip Morris, New York, NY, December 18, 1990 - February, 1991.

Works on Mulberry Paper, 1990 Seoul International Art Festival, The National Museum of Contemporary Art, Seoul, Korea, November 21, 1990 - February 20, 1991. Catalogue, ill. pp. 70 - 71.

Baltimore Collects: Painting and Sculpture Since 1960, Baltimore Museum of Art, Baltimore, MD, June - July 22, 1990.

The 8th International Small Sculpture Triennial of Budapest, 1990, Palace of Budapest, August - December, 1990. Catalogue, ill.

1991

A Selection of Paintings and Sculpture: Nancy Graves, Pat Steir, Sam Francis, Terence La Noue, Ochi Gallery, Sun Valley, Idaho, February 1 - 28, 1991.

El Sueno de Egipto (La Influencia del Arte Egipcio en el Arte Contemporaneo), Centro Cultural Arte Contemporaneo, A.C., Mexico, February - May, 1991, Catalogue, ill. pp. 113 - 114.

IIeme Biennale de Sculpture Montecarlo 1991, Catalogue, ill. p. 53.

Small-Scale Sculpture, Sewell Art Gallery, Rice University, Houston, TX, October 24 - December 14, 1991.

Directions, Marion Locks Gallery, Philadelphia, PA, January 10 - February 23, 1991.

The Inaugural Exhibition - Mary & Crosby Kemper Collection, Kansas City Art Institute, Kansas City, KS, January 13 - February 10, 1991. Catalogue, ill. plate no. 25.

The 166th Annual Exhibition, National Academy of Art and Design, New York, NY, April 1 - May 5, 1991.

Interactions: Collaborations in the Visual and Performing Arts, I.C.A., University of Pennsylvania, Philadelphia, PA, May 22 - July 7, 1991.

Metallics: Art and Craft at Tallix Foundry, The Century Association, New York, NY, May 5 - 31, 1991.

Works on Paper by Gallery Artists, Knoedler & Company, New York, NY, September 7 - October 3, 1991.

Master Drawings, Eugene Binder Galerie, Cologne, Germany, November 15 - December 22, 1991.

1992

The Midtown Flower Show, Midtown Payson Galleries, New York, NY, February 6 - March 7, 1992.

Bibliography

1989

Armstrong, Elizabeth and McGuire, Sheila. *First Impressions: Early Prints by Forty-Six Contemporary Artists.* New York: Hudson Hills Press. (In association with the Walker Art Center, p. 80, color ill. p. 81.)

Russell, John. "Nancy Graves." *The New York Times,* October 13, 1989, p. C24.

Willers, Emil. *The Experience of Landscape: Three Decades of Sculpture.* Exhibition catalogue. New York: Whitney Museum of American Art.

Wright, Jeff. "With and Against Purpose." *COVER*, November 1989, p. 8

Young, Charles. *The Development of Sculptural Form.* Exhibition catalogue. New York: Associated American Artists. pp. 35-45, ill.

1990

Cuperman, Pedro. *Nancy Graves: Icons of Language.* Exhibition catalogue. Stockholm: Heland Wetterling Gallery.

Cyphers, Peggy. "Nancy Graves." *Arts* Magazine, January 1990, p. 95, ill.

Denson, G. Roger. "Nancy Graves: Knoedler." *Flash Art*, January/February 1990, p. 131, ill.

DeVuono, Frances. "Nancy Graves." *ARTnews*, February 1990, p. 152, ill.

Halloway, Memory. "Nancy Graves: Between Painting and Sculpture." *Art International*, Summer 1990, pp. 29-33, ill.

Luebbers, Leslie. *Mind and Matter: New American Abstraction.* Exhibition catalogue. San Francisco: World Print Council. p. 15

Rubinstein, Charlotte Streifer. *American Women Sculptors: A History of Women Working in Three Dimensions.* Boston: G.K. Hall & Co. pp. 453-456, ill.

Simon, Joan. *The 8th International Small Sculpture Triennial of Budapest Palace Exhibition, 1990.* Exhibition catalogue. Budapest: Palace of Exhibitions. pp. 30-35, ill. p. 35

Sutherland Harris, Ann. "Entering the Mainstream: Women Sculptors of the Twentieth Century (Part III: Jackie Winsor & Nancy Graves)." *Gallerie Women Artists.* Number 8, Vol. II, No. 4.

1991

Bourdon, David. *Nancy Graves: The Virtues of Metaphor.* Exhibition catalogue. Philadelphia: Locks Gallery.

Chadwick, Susan. "The Energy of Nancy Graves." *The Houston Post*, April 14, 1991, p. G-13.

Chadwick, Susan. "Brush With Equality." *The Houston Post*, April 16, 1991.

Curtis, Cathy. "Works Mirror Wit, Charm of Metal Sculptor Nancy Graves."*Orange County Calendar*, March 4, 1991, p. F2.

Johnson, Patricia G. "Graves Mixes Art, Science." *Houston Chronicle*, April 23, 1991.

Sozanski, Edward J. "Nancy Graves at Marion Locks." *The Philadelphia Inquirer*, March 21, 1991, p. 3-D.

Stein, Judith. "Nancy Graves at Marion Locks." *Art in America,* December 1991, p. 125, ill.

Wheeler, Daniel. *Art Since Mid-Century; 1945 to the Present.* New York: Vendome Press. pp. 302-303, 321; ill. pp. 294, 302, 303.

1992

Schwan,Gary. "Gallery Honors Graves for Multicultural Works." *The Palm Beach Pôst*, February 21, 1992, p. 22.

Sjostrom, Jan. "The Alchemy of Time." *Palm Beach Daily News*, Sunday, February 9, 1992, p. B1.

Stretch, Bonnie Barrett. "Nancy Graves: Knoedler." *ARTnews*, January 1992, p. 118, ill.